Simply
COLORADO
Too!

More Nutritious Recipes
for Busy People

Colorado Dietetic Association

Simply COLORADO, Too!

Edited, designed, and manufactured
in the United States of America by
Favorite Recipes® Press, an imprint of

FRP

P.O. Box 305142, Nashville, Tennessee 37230
800.358.0560

Managing Editor: Mary Cummings
Art Director: Steve Newman
Project Manager: Debbie Van Mol
Cover Design: Harry Spetnagel—Planet Graphics, Inc.
Book Design: Bruce Gore
Project Production: Sara Anglin

Library of Congress Number: 99-093217
ISBN: 0-9626337-2-0
First Printing: 2000 15,000 copies
Second Printing: 2001 10,000 copies

CONTENTS

PREFACE

Simple, tasty, and healthy recipes for those who don't have much time to cook: This successful formula for a first book has created a demand for another. The Colorado Dietetic Association, the state's leading association for nutrition professionals, has returned with more nutritious recipes for busy people.

Created because of overwhelming demand, *Simply Colorado, Too!* contains cuisine that is not only delicious and healthful but is easy to prepare, using common ingredients found in any kitchen. Each recipe is designed to fit into a healthy lifestyle. While emphasizing flavor and convenience, these recipes have been adapted to be lower-fat, nutrient-rich counterparts to traditional dishes.

This collection of recipes was developed and tested by Colorado's nutrition experts, registered dietitians who are members of the Colorado Dietetic Association. When you want nutrition information or advice, be sure to look for the initials RD after a person's name. This signifies that he/she has at least a bachelor's degree in nutrition, dietetics, or a closely related area from a U.S. regionally accredited college/university and has completed an approved preprofessional work-experience program. RDs demonstrate their knowledge of food and nutrition by passing a national credentialing exam, and they stay on the cutting edge of nutrition information and research by participating in continuing education. The RD is your link to nutrition and health.

Because *Simply Colorado, Too!* recognizes that people want delicious food but don't want to spend hours in the kitchen preparing it, we have designated recipes that can be made in thirty minutes or less with a 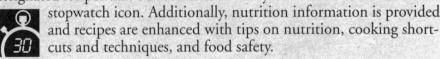 stopwatch icon. Additionally, nutrition information is provided and recipes are enhanced with tips on nutrition, cooking short-cuts and techniques, and food safety.

For all of you who made *Simply Colorado* a mainstay of your cookbook collection, we hope *Simply Colorado, Too!* finds a valued place alongside.

ACKNOWLEDGMENTS

COOKBOOK STEERING COMMITTEE

Cookbook Chairman   Kay Petre Massey, MA, RD
Co-Chairman   Laura Brieser-Smith, RD, MPH

Recipe Testing Committee   Kay Petre Massey, MA, RD
Laura Brieser-Smith, RD, MPH
Tracy Gillespie, RD, MPH

Marketing Committee   Tami Anderson, RD
Mary Lee Chin, RD
Stephanie Smith, MS, RD

Text/Nutrition Tips Editor   Sarah Harding Laidlaw, MS, RD

Area Coordinators   Heidi Fritz, RD   *Denver*
Irene Patrick, RD   *Northern*
Suzanne Mason, RD   *Southern*
Mary Bennett, RD   *Western*

Executive Directors   Karen & Randy Erickson

USING NUTRITION INFORMATION

Each *Simply Colorado, Too!* recipe was selected, first and foremost, because it tastes terrific. The recipes were also chosen because they are lower in fat and calories and higher in essential nutrients than traditional counterparts. While representing healthful cuisine, these recipes are not intended for any specific dietary restriction and should not replace the advice of your physician or registered dietitian.

In the interest of lowering fat, many Americans have forgotten the larger picture, that healthful eating includes a variety of whole foods, whole grains, fresh fruits and vegetables, dairy products, and lean meat. For this reason, we made a conscious choice to include recipes that are not just lower in fat but loaded with nutrients. Additionally, these recipes do not rely heavily on fat-free products to decrease the fat content. We have provided information about each recipe's calorie, fat, carbohydrate, protein, and fiber content. Also, when a recipe is an especially good source of a particular nutrient, we have pointed that out.

The key to better health does not lie within a pantry stocked full of fat-free foods and dietary supplements. The key lies with food—what a surprise. Research has exploded with information about components of food that may reduce the risk of such chronic diseases as heart disease and cancer. These components have been given the name of phytochemicals and new ones are discovered regularly. There's carotene in carrots and lycopene in tomatoes, phytoestrogens in soy and sphingolipids (a type of fat) in milk. You can't possibly capture all of their benefits in a pill.

The Colorado Dietetic Association encourages you to follow the USDA's Food Guide Pyramid as a guideline for evaluating your food intake. The Pyramid is based on research regarding what food Americans eat, what nutrients are in these foods, and how to make the best food choices for you.

The Pyramid will help you choose what and how much to eat from each food group to get the nutrients you need without consuming too many calories. Keep in mind these recommendations are for healthy Americans two years of age or more.

The Pyramid is an outline of what to eat each day. It's not a rigid prescription, but a general guide that lets you choose a healthful diet that's right for you.

FOOD GUIDE PYRAMID

A Guide to Daily Food Choices

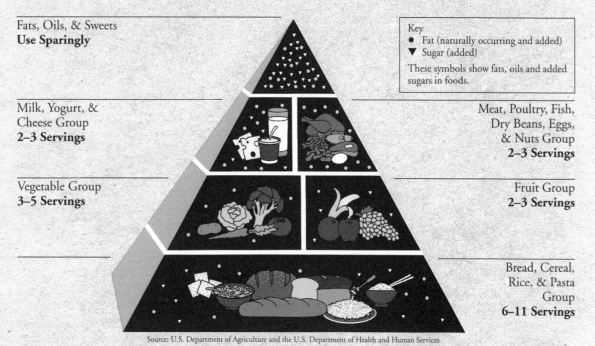

Fats, Oils, & Sweets
Use Sparingly

Key
● Fat (naturally occurring and added)
▼ Sugar (added)
These symbols show fats, oils and added sugars in foods.

Milk, Yogurt, &
Cheese Group
2–3 Servings

Meat, Poultry, Fish,
Dry Beans, Eggs,
& Nuts Group
2–3 Servings

Vegetable Group
3–5 Servings

Fruit Group
2–3 Servings

Bread, Cereal,
Rice, & Pasta
Group
6–11 Servings

Source: U.S. Department of Agriculture and the U.S. Department of Health and Human Services

What Counts as a Serving?

Bread, Cereal, Rice, and Pasta
1 slice bread
1 ounce ready-to-eat cereal
½ cup cooked cereal, rice or pasta

Vegetables
1 cup raw leafy vegetables
½ cup other vegetables, cooked
¾ cup vegetable juice

Fruit
1 medium apple, banana, or orange
½ cup canned, cooked chopped fruit
¾ cup fruit juice

Milk, Yogurt, and Cheese
1 cup milk or yogurt
1½ ounces natural cheese
2 ounces process cheese

Meat, Poultry, Fish, Dry Beans, Eggs, and Nuts
2 to 3 ounces cooked lean meat, poultry or fish
½ cup cooked dry beans, 1 egg or 2 tablespoons
peanut butter count as 1 ounce lean meat

NUTRITIONAL PROFILES

The editors have attempted to present these family recipes in a format that allows approximate nutritional values to be computed. Persons with dietary or health problems or whose diets require close monitoring should not rely solely on the nutritional information provided. They should consult their physician or a registered dietitian for specific information.

Abbreviations for Nutritional Profile

Cal — Calories	T Fat — Total Fat	Sod — Sodium
Prot — Protein	Chol — Cholesterol	g — grams
Carbo — Carbohydrates	Fiber — Dietary Fiber	mg — milligrams

Nutritional information for these recipes is computed from information derived from many sources, including materials supplied by the United States Department of Agriculture, computer databanks, and journals in which the information is assumed to be in the public domain. However, many specialty items, new products, and processed food may not be available from these sources or may vary from the average values used in these profiles. More information on new and/or specific products may be obtained by reading the nutrient labels. Unless otherwise specified, the nutritional profile of these recipes is based on all measurements being level.

- Artificial sweeteners vary in use and strength and should be used to taste, using the recipe ingredients as a guideline. Sweeteners using aspartame (NutraSweet and Equal) should not be used as a sweetener in recipes involving prolonged heating, which reduces the sweet taste. For further information on the use of these sweeteners, refer to the package.
- Alcoholic ingredients have been analyzed for the basic information. Cooking causes the evaporation of alcohol, which decreases alcoholic and caloric content.
- Buttermilk, sour cream, and yogurt are the types available commercially.
- Canned beans and vegetables have been analyzed with the canning liquid. Rinsing and draining canned products will lower the sodium content.
- Chicken, cooked for boning and chopping, has been roasted; this cooking method yields the lowest caloric values.
- Eggs are all large. To avoid raw eggs that may carry salmonella, as in eggnog or 6-week muffin batter, use an equivalent amount of commercial egg substitute.
- Flour is unsifted all-purpose flour.
- Garnishes, serving suggestions, and other optional information and variations are not included in the profile.
- Margarine and butter are regular, not whipped or presoftened.
- Oil is any type of vegetable cooking oil. Shortening is hydrogenated vegetable shortening.
- Salt and other ingredients to taste as noted in the ingredients have not been included in the nutritional profile.
- If a choice of ingredients has been given, the profile reflects the first option. If a choice of amounts has been given, the profile reflects the greater amount.

APPETIZERS

APPETIZERS

Polenta Antipasto	11
Fresh Basil Bruschetta	12
Hot Artichoke Crostini	13
Sun-Dried Tomato Crostini	14
Crab Meat Canapés	15
Snappy Black Bean Dip	16
Hot Pepper Cheese Dip	17
Five-Minute Pesto Dip	17
Southwestern Layered Dip	18
Caponata	19
Smoked Salmon Pâté	20
Mushroom Pâté	21
Baked Chinese Dumplings	21
Marinated Mushrooms	22
Cajun Shrimp	23
Chinese Tortilla Roll-Ups	24

Polenta Antipasto

For an appetizer that looks impressive and is quick to fix, try this tasty antipasto.

1   (1-pound) roll prepared flavored polenta
3   tablespoons freshly grated Parmesan or asiago cheese
     julienned roasted red peppers (optional)
     sautéed sliced mushrooms (optional)
     chopped black olives (optional)
     chopped fresh tomatoes (optional)
     chopped fresh basil (optional)
     pesto sauce (optional)

Cut the polenta into eighteen ¼-inch slices. Arrange the slices in a single layer on a baking sheet sprayed with nonstick cooking spray. Sprinkle each slice with ½ teaspoon of the cheese.

Bake at 350 degrees for 10 to 15 minutes or until light brown and crisp. Cool slightly. Serve plain or top with roasted red peppers, mushrooms, black olives, tomatoes, basil and/or pesto.

Tip: For a special presentation, cut the polenta into different shapes with small cookie cutters or a sharp knife. A shamrock shape spread with basil pesto provides a special look on Saint Patrick's Day; a heart shape topped with roasted red peppers will tie in with your color scheme on Valentine's Day.

YIELD: 18 SERVINGS

Nutrients Per Serving: **Cal 89; Prot 2 g; Carbo 17 g; T Fat 1 g; (Saturated Fat <1 g); Chol 1 mg; Fiber 1 g; Sod 20 mg**

Prepared polenta may be located in a variety of places in your grocery store. You might find it in the refrigerator section with the cheese, on the shelves with health foods or Italian foods, or in the freezer section. A good substitute for prepared polenta is the Savory Polenta on page 155. Spread the polenta in a rectangular or square dish. Chill for eight to ten hours. Cut into small rectangles.

Many fresh herbs can be frozen for use year-round. Separate the herbs into small shoots or leaves, chop with a knife, and pack into four-ounce baby food jars or sealable plastic bags. Store in the freezer. Fresh herbs may also be preserved by processing in a blender or food processor with an equal amount of water. Pour the mixture into ice cube trays, freeze, and then transfer to sealable plastic bags.

Fresh Basil Bruschetta

3	medium tomatoes, chopped
2	tablespoons chopped fresh basil
2	teaspoons olive oil
$\frac{1}{8}$	teaspoon salt
1	baguette French bread, cut into $\frac{1}{2}$-inch slices
2	tablespoons grated Parmesan cheese

Combine the tomatoes, basil, olive oil and salt in a bowl and mix gently. Chill, covered, for 1 to 2 hours to allow the flavors to marry.

Toast the bread in a toaster. Top each slice with some of the tomato mixture. Sprinkle with the cheese. Serve at room temperature or broil just until heated through.

YIELD: 24 SLICES

Nutrients Per Slice: **Cal 61; Prot 2 g; Carbo 11 g; T Fat 1 g; (Saturated Fat <1 g); Chol <1 mg; Fiber 1 g; Sod 138 mg**

Hot Artichoke Crostini

The term crostini means little toasts in Italian. Crostini are small, thin slices of toasted bread that are usually spread with a savory topping. Because it is just toast, there is no fat.

1	baguette French bread
1	cup fat-free mayonnaise
½	cup grated Parmesan cheese
½	cup soft bread crumbs
½	teaspoon spicy Worcestershire sauce
1	(14-ounce) can artichoke hearts, drained, chopped
1	(4-ounce) can chopped green chiles
2	garlic cloves, minced
	ground black pepper to taste
	sliced cherry tomatoes (optional)

Cut the baguette into thirty-six ¼-inch slices. Arrange cut side down on a baking sheet lined with foil. Bake at 400 degrees for 5 minutes or until light brown.

Combine the mayonnaise, Parmesan cheese, bread crumbs and Worcestershire sauce in a bowl and mix well. Stir in the artichokes, chiles and garlic. Spread over the bread slices. Bake at 400 degrees for 5 minutes or until heated through. Top with sliced cherry tomatoes.

YIELD: 36 CROSTINI

Nutrients Per Crostini: Cal 53; Prot 2 g; Carbo 9 g; T Fat 1 g; (Saturated Fat <1 g); Chol 1 mg; Fiber 1 g; Sod 222 mg

Sun-Dried Tomato Crostini

1	ounce sun-dried tomatoes
¼	cup pitted kalamata olives
1	tablespoon capers
1	tablespoon olive oil
2	garlic cloves, minced
1	baguette French bread, cut into ½-inch slices
8	ounces fat-free cream cheese, softened
2	tablespoons julienned fresh basil

Pour boiling water over the sun-dried tomatoes in a heat-resistant bowl to hydrate. Let stand for 2 minutes; drain. Combine the sun-dried tomatoes, olives, capers, olive oil and garlic in a blender or food processor container. Process until blended.

Arrange the bread slices in a single layer on a baking sheet. Bake at 400 degrees for 8 to 10 minutes or until golden brown. Spread the cream cheese on the bread slices. Top with the tomato mixture and sprinkle with the basil. Arrange the crostini on a serving platter. Do not assemble the crostini until just before serving.

Tip: Sun-dried tomatoes make a flavorful addition to recipes. Substitute rehydrated sun-dried tomatoes for the oil-pack version to decrease fat grams. One-third cup oil-pack sun-dried tomatoes contains 24 grams of fat. An equal amount of rehydrated sun-dried tomatoes contains only 1 gram of fat.

YIELD: 24 CROSTINI

Nutrients Per Crostini: **Cal 70; Prot 3 g; Carbo 11 g; T Fat 1 g; (Saturated Fat <1 g); Chol 1 mg; Fiber 1 g; Sod 210 mg**

*F*at-free cream cheese is an excellent low-fat alternative to the higher-fat version. Because of lack of flavor, this product should be paired with other flavorful ingredients. Consume foods with fat-free cream cheese soon after preparation; the cream cheese tends to dry and crack shortly after exposure to air.

Crab Meat Canapés

1	pound fresh crab meat, flaked
2	green onions, finely chopped
3	tablespoons chopped fresh dillweed
2	tablespoons pine nuts, toasted
2	teaspoons lemon zest
¼	teaspoon cayenne pepper, or to taste
½	cup fat-free mayonnaise
2	unpeeled cucumbers, scored, sliced
	paprika to taste

Combine the crab meat, green onions, dillweed, pine nuts, lemon zest and cayenne pepper in a bowl and mix gently. Stir in the mayonnaise. Chill, covered, for 1 hour.

Mound some of the crab meat mixture onto each cucumber slice. Arrange the cucumber rounds on a serving platter. Sprinkle with paprika.

Tip: Spoon the crab meat mixture into a small bowl and if time is of the essence, just serve with assorted party crackers.

YIELD: 24 SERVINGS

Nutrients Per Serving: Cal 28; Prot 4 g; Carbo 2 g; T Fat 1 g; (Saturated Fat <1 g); Chol 15 mg; Fiber <1 g; Sod 91 mg

Beans are a good source of fiber, and fiber is fabulous! Fiber helps lower blood cholesterol, control blood sugar fluctuations, and promote bowel regularity. It can also help reduce your risk of heart disease, some cancers, and intestinal problems.

Snappy Black Bean Dip

1	(15-ounce) can black beans, drained, rinsed
1	teaspoon vegetable oil
½	cup chopped onion
2	garlic cloves, minced
½	cup chopped tomato
⅓	cup picante sauce
½	teaspoon cumin
½	teaspoon chili powder
¼	cup shredded reduced-fat Monterey Jack cheese
¼	cup chopped fresh cilantro
1	tablespoon fresh lime juice

 Mash the black beans in a bowl. Heat the oil in a large skillet over medium heat. Add the onion and garlic. Sauté until golden brown. Stir in the black beans, tomato, picante sauce, cumin and chili powder. Cook for 5 minutes or until thickened, stirring occasionally. Remove from heat. Add the cheese, cilantro and lime juice, stirring until the cheese melts. Serve with baked tortilla chips.

YIELD: 16 (2-TABLESPOON) SERVINGS

Nutrients Per Serving: Cal 34; Prot 2 g; Carbo 5 g; T Fat 1 g; (Saturated Fat <1 g); Chol 1 mg; Fiber 2 g; Sod 121 mg

Hot Pepper Cheese Dip

8	ounces tub-style reduced-fat cream cheese
1	cup shredded reduced-fat Jalapeño/Monterey Jack cheese
⅓	cup skim milk
⅓	cup finely chopped red bell pepper
¼	cup finely chopped celery
⅛	teaspoon garlic powder
1	to 3 drops of hot pepper sauce, or to taste

Combine the cream cheese, Monterey Jack cheese and skim milk in a bowl and mix well. Stir in the red pepper, celery, garlic powder and hot pepper sauce.

Chill, covered, for 1 to 2 hours to allow the flavors to marry. Serve with fresh vegetables and/or assorted party crackers.

YIELD: 14 (2-TABLESPOON) SERVINGS

Nutrients Per Serving: Cal 62; Prot 4 g; Carbo 2 g; T Fat 4 g;
(Saturated Fat 3 g); Chol 12 mg; Fiber <1 g; Sod 133 mg

Five-Minute Pesto Dip

Adults need one thousand to twelve hundred milligrams of calcium daily. This recipe gives you a good start toward reaching that amount.

1	cup hot water
⅓	cup chopped sun-dried tomatoes
1	cup plain fat-free yogurt
¼	cup pesto sauce

 Pour the hot water over the sun-dried tomatoes in a bowl to hydrate. Let stand for 5 minutes; drain.

Combine the sun-dried tomatoes, yogurt and pesto sauce in a bowl and mix well. Chill, covered, in the refrigerator. Serve with fresh vegetables.

YIELD: 12 (2-TABLESPOON) SERVINGS

Nutrients Per Serving: Cal 42; Prot 2 g; Carbo 4 g; T Fat 3g;
(Saturated Fat 1 g); Chol 2 mg; Fiber <1 g; Sod 109 mg

Southwestern Layered Dip

A wonderfully easy appetizer to take to your next Bronco party!

1	(15-ounce) can black beans, rinsed, drained
1	(4-ounce) can chopped black olives, drained
1	small onion, finely chopped
2	tablespoons fresh lime juice
1	tablespoon olive oil
1	garlic clove, minced
¼	teaspoon crushed red pepper
¼	teaspoon cumin
¼	teaspoon salt
⅛	teaspoon black pepper
8	ounces tub-style reduced-fat cream cheese
⅔	cup chopped tomato
⅓	cup chopped green onions

Combine the black beans, black olives, onion, lime juice, olive oil, garlic, red pepper, cumin, salt and black pepper in a bowl and mix well. Chill, covered, for 2 hours or longer.

Spread the cream cheese evenly on a 10-inch round serving plate. Spread the bean mixture over the cream cheese. Arrange the tomato in a ring around the outer edge. Sprinkle with the green onions. Serve with baked tortilla chips or reduced-fat crackers.

Tip: Traditional tortilla chips contain 6 grams of fat per serving, while the baked tortilla chips have only 1 gram of fat per serving.

YIELD: 10 SERVINGS

Nutrients Per Serving: Cal 115; Prot 5 g; Carbo 10 g; T Fat 7 g; (Saturated Fat 3 g); Chol 11 mg; Fiber 3 g; Sod 396 mg

*E*asy Ways to Increase Calcium Intake:
*
Add dry milk powder to mashed potatoes, casseroles, soups, and sauces.
*
Add dry milk powder to rolled oats or other hot cereals before adding water (or milk) and cooking.
*
Drink calcium-fortified orange juice.
*
Consume more yogurt; it contains more calcium than eight ounces of milk. →

Caponata

This eggplant appetizer can be served on crackers, heated on pizza rounds, or used as a pasta sauce.

1	pound eggplant
¼	cup pine nuts
1	green or red bell pepper, chopped
1	medium onion, chopped
2	garlic cloves, minced
2	tablespoons olive oil
1	(16-ounce) can diced tomatoes
1	(4-ounce) can sliced black olives, drained
2	tablespoons red wine vinegar
1	tablespoon capers
2	teaspoons basil
1	teaspoon sugar

Cut the eggplant into ½-inch slices. Spray both sides of the eggplant with nonstick cooking spray. Arrange the slices in a single layer on a baking sheet. Broil until brown on both sides, turning once. Let stand until cool.

Spread the pine nuts on a baking sheet. Toast at 325 degrees until golden brown, stirring occasionally.

Peel the eggplant. Cut the eggplant into ½-inch cubes. Sauté the eggplant, green pepper, onion and garlic in the olive oil in a heavy skillet for 15 minutes or until the vegetables are tender. Stir in the undrained tomatoes, black olives, wine vinegar, capers, basil and sugar. Cook for 10 minutes, stirring occasionally. Spoon into a serving bowl. Sprinkle with the pine nuts. Serve with assorted party crackers. Serve Caponata warm or at room temperature.

YIELD: 40 (2-TABLESPOON) SERVINGS

Nutrients Per Serving: Cal 22; Prot 1 g; Carbo 2 g; T Fat 1 g; (Saturated Fat <1 g); Chol 0 mg; Fiber 1 g; Sod 51 mg

*
Eat calcium-rich vegetables such as kale or Chinese cabbage and broccoli.
*
Include canned sardines and canned salmon (with bones), which also supply heart-healthy omega-3 fatty acids.
*
Use calcium-fortified reduced-fat soy and tofu products.
*
Eat calcium-fortified cereals topped with dried figs.

Smoked Salmon Pâté

¼ cup chopped pecans

1 (14-ounce) can salmon, drained

8 ounces tub-style reduced-fat cream cheese

2 tablespoons grated onion

1 tablespoon lemon juice

1 teaspoon prepared horseradish

¼ teaspoon salt

¼ teaspoon liquid smoke

¼ cup finely chopped fresh parsley

Spread the pecans in a single layer on a baking sheet. Toast at 350 degrees for 5 minutes or until light brown and fragrant. Let stand until cool.

Mash the salmon in a bowl. Add the cream cheese, onion, lemon juice, horseradish, salt and liquid smoke and mix well. Chill, covered, for 15 minutes.

Shape the salmon mixture into a ball. Coat with the parsley. Sprinkle the pecans over the top of the ball and press lightly. Chill, wrapped in plastic wrap, until serving time. Serve with reduced-fat crackers.

Tip: Reduced-fat cream cheese in a tub saves approximately 8 grams of fat over reduced-fat cream cheese packaged as a block.

YIELD: 12 (2-TABLESPOON) SERVINGS

Nutrients Per Serving: Cal 108; Prot 9 g; Carbo 2 g; T Fat 6 g; (Saturated Fat 3 g); Chol 22 mg; Fiber <1 g; Sod 300 mg

Mushroom Pâté

8   ounces fresh mushrooms, chopped
1   medium onion, chopped
1   tablespoon butter
1   teaspoon each Worcestershire sauce and lemon juice
¼   teaspoon salt
⅛   teaspoon pepper
2   tablespoons reduced-fat mayonnaise

Sauté the mushrooms and onion in the butter in a skillet over medium heat until tender. Stir in the next 4 ingredients. Cook for 15 minutes or until the liquid has evaporated.

Process the mushroom mixture in a blender or food processor until smooth. Stir in the mayonnaise. Spoon into a serving bowl. Chill, covered. Serve with party crackers.

YIELD: 8 (2-TABLESPOON) SERVINGS

Nutrients Per Serving: Cal 38; Prot 1 g; Carbo 3 g; T Fat 3 g;
(Saturated Fat 1 g); Chol 4 mg; Fiber 1 g; Sod 122 mg

Baked Chinese Dumplings

6   ounces reduced-fat sausage
¼   cup finely chopped water chestnuts
2   green onions, minced
1   tablespoon reduced-sodium soy sauce
16   won ton wrappers
⅓   cup sweet-and-sour sauce

Brown the sausage in a skillet, stirring until crumbly; drain. Stir in the next 3 ingredients. Cook for 3 minutes. Moisten the edges of the won ton wrappers with water. Spoon a small amount of the sausage mixture in the center of each wrapper. Fold to form a triangle. Press the edges to seal.

Arrange the dumplings in a single layer on a baking sheet sprayed with nonstick cooking spray. Bake at 325 degrees for 10 to 15 minutes or just until crisp. Serve with the sweet-and-sour sauce.

YIELD: 16 SERVINGS

Nutrients Per Serving: Cal 47; Prot 2 g; Carbo 9 g; T Fat <1 g;
(Saturated Fat <1 g); Chol 3 mg; Fiber 3 g; Sod 158 mg

Marinated Mushrooms

1   cup white wine vinegar
1   cup reduced-sodium chicken broth
1½ pounds small mushrooms, trimmed
1   cup reduced-fat Italian salad dressing
1   teaspoon Italian seasoning

Combine the wine vinegar and broth in a saucepan. Bring to a boil. Stir in the mushrooms. Boil for 2 minutes. Drain, reserving ½ cup of the liquid. Cool the mushrooms to room temperature.

Combine the reserved liquid, salad dressing and Italian seasoning in a bowl and mix well. Add the mushrooms and mix gently. Marinate, covered, in the refrigerator for 2 to 10 hours. The flavor of the mushrooms is enhanced with a longer marinating time.

Tip: For a tasty fat-free Italian salad dressing, combine the fat-free Italian salad dressing mix, ½ cup red wine vinegar or balsamic vinegar, and ½ cup water. This product, as most commercially prepared salad dressing mixes, is high in sodium but a small amount goes a long way.

YIELD: 20 SERVINGS

Nutrients Per Serving: Cal 19; Prot 1 g; Carbo 2 g; T Fat <1 g; (Saturated Fat <1 g); Chol <1 mg; Fiber <1 g; Sod 206 mg
Nutritional information includes the entire amount of marinade.

No matter how careful you are about your food choices, don't over-look the importance of physical activity. It promotes a feeling of well-being, reduces stress, lowers risk for some diseases, and burns calories.

Cajun Shrimp

2	tablespoons fresh lemon juice
2	tablespoons chopped fresh parsley
1	tablespoon Cajun spice
1	tablespoon honey
1	tablespoon soy sauce
1	teaspoon extra-virgin olive oil
	cayenne pepper to taste
1	pound large shrimp, peeled, deveined

Combine the lemon juice, parsley, Cajun spice, honey, soy sauce, olive oil and cayenne pepper in a sealable plastic bag. Add the shrimp and seal tightly. Toss to coat. Marinate in the refrigerator for 1 hour, turning occasionally.

Heat a nonstick skillet over medium heat until hot. Add the shrimp and marinade. Sauté until the shrimp turn pink. Serve with lemon wedges.

YIELD: 4 SERVINGS

Nutrients Per Serving: Cal 104; Prot 15 g; Carbo 6 g; T Fat 2 g; (Saturated Fat <1 g); Chol 135 mg; Fiber <1 g; Sod 840 mg

Chinese Tortilla Roll-Ups

8	ounces deveined peeled steamed shrimp
1	tablespoon Chinese five-spice powder
8	ounces fat-free cream cheese
2	garlic cloves, minced
6	(10-inch) flour tortillas
18	large fresh spinach leaves
1	cup julienned roasted red peppers
1	medium avocado, thinly sliced (optional)

Combine the shrimp and Chinese five-spice powder in a sealable plastic bag and seal tightly. Shake to coat. Chill for 1 hour. Chop the shrimp into small pieces.

Combine the cream cheese and garlic in a bowl and mix well. Spread some of the cream cheese mixture on 1 side of each tortilla. Top each tortilla with 3 of the spinach leaves.

Divide the shrimp, red peppers and avocado into 6 equal portions. Arrange 1 portion of the shrimp, 1 portion of the red peppers and 1 portion of the avocado on each tortilla. Roll to enclose the filling. Cut each tortilla roll into 6 pieces. Secure with wooden picks.

YIELD: 36 SERVINGS

Nutrients Per Serving: Cal 57; Prot 4 g; Carbo 8 g; T Fat 1 g; (Saturated Fat <1 g); Chol 13 mg; Fiber 1 g; Sod 154 mg

*F*or a quick snack or an easy appetizer, roll your favorite sandwich fixings in a tortilla. Eat it whole or slice into rounds for appetizers. A mixture of fat-free cream cheese and salsa on whole wheat or garlic tortillas makes a quick-and-easy appetizer.

BRUNCH

BRUNCH

At-Home Cappuccino

This recipe, obtained from the Western Dairy Council, tastes as good as a cappuccino from those fancy coffeehouses.

2   cups skim milk
1   tablespoon sugar
2   cups freshly brewed strong coffee
     cinnamon to taste

 Pour the skim milk into a microwave-safe measuring cup. Microwave on High for 2 minutes and 20 seconds. Pour into a blender container. Add the sugar. Process at high speed for 1 minute or until frothy.
     Pour equal portions of the coffee into 4 mugs. Top each serving with some of the frothy milk. Sprinkle with cinnamon. Serve immediately.

YIELD: 4 SERVINGS

Nutrients Per Serving: **Cal 57; Prot 4 g; Carbo 10 g; T Fat <1 g; (Saturated Fat <1 g); Chol 2 mg; Fiber 0 g; Sod 65 mg**

Palisade Peach Smoothie

1   cup peach fat-free yogurt
¾   cup peach nectar
1½   cups frozen sliced unsweetened peaches
½   cup frozen unsweetened raspberries

 Combine the yogurt and peach nectar in a blender container. Process until blended. Add the peaches and raspberries. Process until smooth. Serve immediately.

YIELD: 1 SERVING

Nutrients Per Serving: **Cal 478; Prot 11 g; Carbo 105 g; T Fat 2 g; (Saturated Fat <1 g); Chol 5 mg; Fiber 13 g; Sod 130 mg**

Fruit with Orange Yogurt Dip

¾ cup orange reduced-fat yogurt
2 tablespoons brown sugar
1 teaspoon grated orange zest
2 cups sliced unpeeled apples

Combine the yogurt, brown sugar and orange zest in a serving bowl and mix well. Chill, covered, for 1 hour. Arrange the apples around the dip on a serving plate. May substitute your favorite fruit for the apples.

Tip: Fruits are a nutritional gold mine, loaded with vitamin A, vitamin C, potassium, and fiber. Just ½ of a cantaloupe provides 86 percent of your daily vitamin A needs and almost 200 percent of your daily vitamin C needs.

YIELD: 4 SERVINGS

Nutrients Per Serving: **Cal 122; Prot 2 g; Carbo 28 g; T Fat 1 g; (Saturated Fat <1 g); Chol 4 mg; Fiber 2 g; Sod 27mg**

Calcium is bone food. It also builds strong and beautiful teeth and may help control blood pressure and lower the risk of several diseases. The milk group is a great source of calcium as well as protein, B-vitamins, potassium, and magnesium.

The Best Granola

For active people, this makes a great high-energy, nutrient-packed breakfast.

3	cups rolled oats
½	cup walnut pieces
½	cup unsweetened shredded coconut
½	cup blanched almond halves
¼	cup sunflower kernels
¼	cup maple syrup
¼	cup honey
¼	cup canola oil
½	cup chopped dried apricots
½	cup raisins

Combine the oats, walnuts, coconut, almonds and sunflower kernels in a bowl and mix well. Mix the maple syrup, honey and canola oil in a saucepan. Cook until heated through, stirring frequently. Pour over the oat mixture and stir until coated.

Spread the oat mixture evenly on a baking sheet. Bake at 325 degrees for 15 minutes or until golden brown, stirring and respreading every 5 minutes. Remove from oven. Stir in the apricots and raisins. Transfer to a clean baking sheet. Let stand until cool; crumble. Store in an airtight container.

Tip: Oats are a good source of water-soluble fiber, the kind that helps lower blood cholesterol.

YIELD: 16 SERVINGS

Nutrients Per Serving: Cal 248; Prot 6 g; Carbo 28 g; T Fat 15 g; (Saturated Fat 3 g); Chol 0 mg; Fiber 4 g; Sod 5 mg

Mexicana Cheese Pie

1	cup fat-free cottage cheese
½	cup fat-free sour cream
2	eggs
2	egg whites
1	teaspoon cumin
¼	teaspoon garlic powder
¼	teaspoon onion powder
1	(4-ounce) can chopped green chiles, drained
½	cup shredded Monterey Jack cheese
½	cup shredded Colby cheese
1	large flour tortilla wrap or 3 (8-inch) flour tortillas
	salsa (optional)

Place the cottage cheese in a strainer; drain. Combine the sour cream, eggs, egg whites, cumin, garlic powder and onion powder in a bowl. Whisk until blended. Stir in the cottage cheese, chiles, Monterey Jack cheese and Colby cheese.

Fit the tortilla wrap into a 9-inch pie plate. Pour the cottage cheese mixture into the prepared pie plate. Bake at 375 degrees for 40 to 45 minutes or until a knife inserted in the center comes out clean. Let stand for 5 minutes before serving. Top with salsa.

YIELD: 6 SERVINGS

Nutrients Per Serving: Cal 234; Prot 16 g; Carbo 20 g; T Fat 9 g; (Saturated Fat 5 g); Chol 91 mg; Fiber 1 g; Sod 647 mg

Nutrition science has evolved and it is now understood that it is not only the intake of dietary cholesterol, but also of saturated fat, that is the major dietary factor affecting blood cholesterol levels. Elevated blood cholesterol remains a major risk factor that leads to cardiovascular disease.

Omelet Sandwiches On-the-Run

These breakfast sandwiches will become a favorite to enjoy as you rush to work or to the ski slopes.

½   cup chopped green bell pepper
½   cup chopped onion
1   teaspoon canola oil
6   eggs, beaten
¼   cup skim milk
      salt and pepper to taste
1   cup shredded reduced-fat sharp Cheddar cheese
1   cup chopped ham
8   English muffins, split, toasted

Sauté the green pepper and onion in the canola oil in nonstick skillet until tender. Whisk the eggs, skim milk, salt and pepper in a bowl until blended. Stir in the green pepper mixture.

   Pour the egg mixture into a 9x9-inch baking pan sprayed with nonstick cooking spray. Sprinkle with the cheese and ham. Bake at 425 degrees for 20 minutes or until set. Let stand for 10 minutes. Cut into 8 equal portions. Place 1 portion on the bottom half of each English muffin. Top with the remaining halves. May substitute split toasted bagels for the English muffins.

   Tip: You can prepare Omelet Sandwiches in advance and freeze for future use. To reheat, wrap each frozen sandwich in a paper towel. Microwave on Medium for 3½ to 4 minutes. Or, wrap in foil and bake at 350 degrees for 20 to 25 minutes or until heated through.

YIELD: 8 SANDWICHES

Nutrients Per Sandwich: Cal 272; Prot 18 g; Carbo 29 g; T Fat 9 g;
(Saturated Fat 3 g); Chol 177 mg; Fiber 2 g; Sod 640 mg

Miner's Potato and Ham Frittata

Great for a brunch or served with a salad for dinner.

2	medium red potatoes
1	teaspoon olive oil
4	green onions, chopped
1	garlic clove, minced
4	eggs, beaten
4	egg whites, beaten
$\frac{3}{4}$	cup chopped lean ham
	salt and pepper to taste
$\frac{1}{4}$	cup shredded sharp Cheddar cheese

Pierce each potato twice with a fork. Microwave on High for $2\frac{1}{2}$ minutes; turn. Microwave for $2\frac{1}{2}$ minutes longer. Cut into thin slices. Cool for 10 minutes.

Heat the olive oil in a 10-inch ovenproof nonstick skillet. Add the green onions. Sauté until tender. Stir in the garlic. Sauté for 1 minute longer. Mix the green onion mixture, eggs, egg whites, ham, salt and pepper in a bowl. Pour into the nonstick skillet. (The skillet should be well oiled from cooking the green onions, but coat with nonstick cooking spray if more oil is required.) Layer with the potatoes.

Cook over medium-low heat for 5 to 7 minutes or until the edge is set and the frittata is brown on the bottom. Broil 6 inches from heat source for 2 to 3 minutes or just until set. Sprinkle with the cheese. Run a knife around the edge to loosen the frittata. Slide onto a platter. Cut into 4 wedges. Serve immediately.

Tip: In most recipes, 1 egg can be replaced with 2 egg whites. Egg substitutes without cholesterol and fat can also be an alternative. The usual conversion is $\frac{1}{4}$ cup egg substitute for 1 egg, or check the package for specific directions.

YIELD: 4 SERVINGS

Nutrients Per Serving: Cal 242; Prot 20 g; Carbo 18 g; T Fat 10 g;
(Saturated Fat 4 g); Chol 234 mg; Fiber 2 g; Sod 517 mg

Tofu Breakfast Scramble

An easy way to add more soy-based foods to your diet.

1	pound firm tofu, crumbled
1	teaspoon olive oil
⅓	cup chopped red bell pepper
4	mushrooms, chopped
3	green onions, sliced
2	garlic cloves, minced
2	eggs, beaten
1	tablespoon freshly grated Parmesan cheese
½	teaspoon Italian seasoning
¼	teaspoon salt
⅛	teaspoon pepper

Drain the tofu in a colander. Heat the olive oil in a large nonstick skillet until hot. Add the red pepper, mushrooms, green onions and garlic. Sauté for 5 minutes or until the vegetables are tender.

Combine the tofu, eggs, cheese, Italian seasoning, salt and pepper in a bowl and mix well. Stir into the vegetable mixture. Cook over medium heat for 5 to 10 minutes or until the eggs are cooked through and of the desired consistency, stirring constantly. Serve immediately.

Tip: Spoon the tofu scramble into warm flour tortillas and serve with salsa for a Southwestern touch.

YIELD: 4 SERVINGS

Nutrients Per Serving: Cal 137; Prot 13 g; Carbo 6 g; T Fat 7 g; (Saturated Fat 2 g); Chol 107 mg; Fiber 1 g; Sod 249 mg

It is too early to know the extent to which soy or its isoflavones can reduce the risk of breast or prostate cancer, osteoporosis, or hot flashes. The research and evidence is encouraging, but still preliminary. What we do know is that a soy product like tofu is a good source of protein that contains no cholesterol and less saturated fat than poultry or meat.

Alpine Baked Oatmeal

A hearty and warm breakfast for cold mornings.

When choosing cereals, get the most from your food dollar by choosing those with the following attributes: whole grain cereals with whole grain listed as the first ingredient; no more than three grams of fat per serving; the first three ingredients on the ingredients panel do not include sugar or any type of sugar; and at least three grams of fiber per serving.

3	cups quick-cooking or old-fashioned oats
½	cup packed brown sugar
2	teaspoons baking powder
½	teaspoon cinnamon
½	teaspoon salt
1	cup skim milk
½	cup unsweetened applesauce
1	egg, lightly beaten
1	teaspoon vanilla extract
½	cup chopped drained canned peaches

Combine the oats, brown sugar, baking powder, cinnamon and salt in a bowl and mix well. Stir in the skim milk, applesauce, egg and vanilla. Fold in the peaches.

Spread the peach mixture in a 1½-quart baking dish or 9x9-inch baking pan sprayed with nonstick cooking spray. Bake at 350 degrees for 30 to 35 minutes. Serve with vanilla fat-free yogurt or skim milk.

YIELD: 6 SERVINGS

Nutrients Per Serving: Cal 308; Prot 10 g; Carbo 58 g; T Fat 4 g; (Saturated Fat 1 g); Chol 36 mg; Fiber 5 g; Sod 398 mg

Baked Breakfast Apples

This deceptively easy recipe makes a delicious, warm start to a cold morning.

4   large Golden Delicious apples, cored
½   cup packed brown sugar
½   teaspoon cinnamon
1   cup apple juice
2   cups vanilla fat-free yogurt
1   cup reduced-fat granola

Arrange the apples in a round baking dish. Combine the brown sugar and cinnamon in a bowl and mix well. Spoon some of the brown sugar mixture into each apple cavity and sprinkle the remaining brown sugar mixture over the top of the apples. Pour the apple juice into the baking dish.

    Bake at 350 degrees for 50 to 60 minutes or until the apples are tender when pierced with a sharp knife, basting every 15 minutes. Place the apples in individual dessert bowls. Cut each apple to but not through into 8 wedges to resemble a flower. Fill the center of each apple with ½ cup of the yogurt. Sprinkle with the granola.

YIELD: 4 SERVINGS

Nutrients Per Serving: Cal 460; Prot 9 g; Carbo 107 g; T Fat 3 g; (Saturated Fat <1 g); Chol 2 mg; Fiber 7 g; Sod 142 mg

Cinnamon Bubble Bread

An impressive reduced-fat breakfast treat. The whole wheat dough is a good source of fiber.

2	(1-pound) loaves frozen whole wheat bread dough
1	cup sugar
1/3	cup packed brown sugar
1/4	cup skim milk
1	tablespoon margarine
1	tablespoon cinnamon
2	tablespoons sugar
1	teaspoon cinnamon

Thaw the bread dough in the refrigerator for 8 to 10 hours. Combine 1 cup sugar, brown sugar, skim milk, margarine and 1 tablespoon cinnamon in a small saucepan. Bring to a boil. Boil for 1 minute, stirring frequently. Remove from heat. Cool for 10 minutes.

Cut each bread loaf into 24 equal portions with kitchen shears or a sharp knife. Mix 2 tablespoons sugar and 1 teaspoon cinnamon in a shallow dish. Roll each bread portion in the sugar mixture. Layer the bread pieces in a 12-cup bundt pan sprayed with nonstick cooking spray. Pour the syrup over the prepared layers.

Let rise, covered, in a warm place for 35 minutes or until doubled in bulk; remove cover. Bake at 350 degrees for 25 minutes or until light brown. Run a sharp knife around the edge of the pan. Invert onto a serving plate. Let stand for 5 minutes before serving.

YIELD: 18 SERVINGS

Nutrients Per Serving: Cal 196; Prot 5 g; Carbo 40 g; T Fat 3 g;
(Saturated Fat 1 g); Chol <1 mg; Fiber 4 g; Sod 277 mg

Pear Walnut Coffee Cake

BROWN SUGAR TOPPING

¼   cup packed brown sugar
1   tablespoon butter, softened
¾   teaspoon cinnamon
¼   cup chopped walnuts

COFFEE CAKE

½   cup all-purpose flour
½   cup whole wheat flour
½   teaspoon baking powder
½   teaspoon baking soda
¼   teaspoon salt
½   cup sugar
3   tablespoons butter, softened
1   egg
1   teaspoon vanilla extract
½   cup fat-free sour cream
1½ cups chopped peeled pears

For the topping, combine the brown sugar, butter and cinnamon in a bowl and mix well. Stir in the walnuts.

For the coffee cake, mix the all-purpose flour, whole wheat flour, baking powder, baking soda and salt in a bowl. Beat the sugar and butter in a mixer bowl until light and fluffy. Add the egg and vanilla, beating until blended. Add the flour mixture alternately with the sour cream, mixing just until blended after each addition.

Spoon half the batter into an 8x8-inch baking pan sprayed with nonstick cooking spray. Spread with the pears. Top with the remaining batter. Sprinkle with the topping.

Bake at 350 degrees for 35 to 40 minutes or until a wooden pick inserted in the center comes out clean and the top is brown.

YIELD: 9 SERVINGS

Nutrients Per Serving: Cal 235; Prot 4 g; Carbo 39 g; T Fat 8 g; (Saturated Fat 4 g); Chol 37 mg; Fiber 2 g; Sod 234 mg

Raspberry Almond Coffee Cake

1	cup raspberries
3	tablespoons brown sugar
½	cup all-purpose flour
½	cup whole wheat flour
⅓	cup sugar
½	teaspoon baking powder
¼	teaspoon baking soda
⅛	teaspoon salt
½	cup plain fat-free yogurt
2	tablespoons margarine, melted
1	teaspoon vanilla extract
1	egg
1	tablespoon slivered almonds

Combine the raspberries and brown sugar in a bowl and toss to mix. Combine the all-purpose flour, whole wheat flour, sugar, baking powder, baking soda and salt in a bowl and mix well. Mix the yogurt, margarine, vanilla and egg in a bowl.

Add the yogurt mixture to the flour mixture, stirring just until moistened. Spread ⅔ of the batter in an 8-inch round baking pan sprayed with nonstick cooking spray. Sprinkle with the raspberry mixture. Spread with the remaining batter. Sprinkle with the almonds.

Bake at 350 degrees for 40 minutes or until a wooden pick inserted in the center comes out clean. Cool on a wire rack for 10 minutes before serving.

YIELD: 8 SERVINGS

Nutrients Per Serving: **Cal 160; Prot 4 g; Carbo 28 g; T Fat 4 g; (Saturated Fat 1 g); Chol 27 mg; Fiber 2 g; Sod 158 mg**

Banana-Stuffed French Toast

1   cup mashed banana
½   teaspoon lemon juice
1   (16-ounce) loaf French bread
1   cup skim milk
2   eggs, beaten
2   egg whites, beaten
2   tablespoons brown sugar
2   teaspoons vanilla extract
½   teaspoon cinnamon

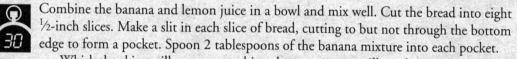

Combine the banana and lemon juice in a bowl and mix well. Cut the bread into eight ½-inch slices. Make a slit in each slice of bread, cutting to but not through the bottom edge to form a pocket. Spoon 2 tablespoons of the banana mixture into each pocket.

Whisk the skim milk, eggs, egg whites, brown sugar, vanilla and cinnamon in a shallow dish. Dip both sides of each filled bread slice into the egg mixture. Cook each slice on a lightly greased hot griddle until golden brown on both sides. Remove to a heated platter. Serve with warm maple syrup.

Tip: Use egg substitutes when making French toast. These reduce the fat and cholesterol in the recipe and give a nice brown crust to the finished product.

YIELD: 4 SERVINGS

Nutrients Per Serving: Cal 455; Prot 18 g; Carbo 82 g; T Fat 6 g;
(Saturated Fat 2 g); Chol 107 mg; Fiber 5 g; Sod 784 mg

Buttermilk Pancakes with Good Morning Mango Sauce

GOOD MORNING MANGO SAUCE

1	large ripe mango, peeled, sliced
¼	cup orange juice
1	teaspoon honey
⅛	teaspoon nutmeg

BUTTERMILK PANCAKES

1½	cups flour
3	tablespoons sugar
1½	teaspoons baking powder
½	teaspoon each baking soda and salt
1½	cups low-fat buttermilk
1	tablespoon canola oil
1	egg
2	egg whites
½	teaspoon vanilla extract

For the sauce, combine the mango, orange juice and honey in a food processor container. Process until smooth. Stir in the nutmeg.

For the pancakes, combine the flour, sugar, baking powder, baking soda and salt in a bowl and mix well. Whisk the buttermilk, canola oil, egg, egg whites and vanilla in a bowl until blended. Add to the flour mixture, stirring just until moistened.

Spray a nonstick skillet with nonstick cooking spray. Heat the skillet over medium heat. Pour ¼ cup of the batter at a time into skillet. Bake until bubbles appear on the surface and begin to burst and the underside is golden brown. Turn the pancakes over. Bake until golden brown. Remove to a heated platter. Serve the pancakes topped with Good Morning Mango Sauce.

YIELD: 8 SERVINGS

Nutrients Per Serving: Cal 178; Prot 6 g; Carbo 32 g; T Fat 3 g; (Saturated Fat 1 g); Chol 28 mg; Fiber 1 g; Sod 387 mg

Mangoes are a superior source of vitamin A and vitamin C, as well as a very good source of potassium and fiber. The best way to choose a ripe mango is to smell the stem ends and choose one with a pleasant scent. Ripen green fruits at room temperature until tender and aromatic.

Granolaberry Pancakes

The granola adds a hearty texture to this old favorite. Great when topped with yogurt.

¾	cup whole wheat flour
1	teaspoon baking powder
½	teaspoon baking soda
½	teaspoon salt
1	cup low-fat buttermilk
1	egg, beaten
1	tablespoon canola oil
1	tablespoon brown sugar
½	cup reduced-fat granola with raisins
½	cup frozen or fresh blueberries

Combine the whole wheat flour, baking powder, baking soda and salt in a bowl and mix well. Whisk the buttermilk, egg, canola oil and brown sugar in a bowl. Add the flour mixture and mix well. Fold in the granola and blueberries.

Pour ¼ cup of the batter at a time onto a hot griddle sprayed with nonstick cooking spray. Bake until bubbles appear on the surface and begin to burst and the underside is golden brown. Turn the pancakes over. Bake until golden brown. Transfer to a heated platter. Serve with vanilla yogurt.

YIELD: 4 SERVINGS

Nutrients Per Serving: **Cal 221; Prot 8 g; Carbo 35 g; T Fat 6 g; (Saturated Fat 1 g); Chol 55 mg; Fiber 4 g; Sod 683 mg**

Trailside Multigrain Pancakes

1	cup old-fashioned oats
1	cup dry multigrain hot cereal
½	cup flour
2	tablespoons sugar
1	teaspoon baking powder
1	teaspoon baking soda
1	teaspoon cinnamon
2	cups low-fat buttermilk
¼	cup unsweetened applesauce
1	egg
1	egg white
	chopped nuts (optional)
	raisins (optional)

Combine the oats, multigrain cereal, flour, sugar, baking powder, baking soda and cinnamon in a bowl and mix well. Mix the buttermilk, applesauce, egg and egg white in a bowl. Add the oats mixture and stir just until moistened. Fold in the nuts and raisins.

Pour ¼ cup of the batter at a time onto a hot griddle sprayed with nonstick cooking spray. Bake until bubbles appear on the surface and begin to burst and the underside is golden brown. Turn the pancakes over. Bake until golden brown. Transfer to a heated platter. Serve with syrup, sliced fruit and/or hot fruit compote.

YIELD: 8 SERVINGS

Nutrients Per Serving: Cal 180; Prot 8 g; Carbo 32 g; T Fat 3 g; (Saturated Fat 1 g); Chol 29 mg; Fiber 2 g; Sod 496 mg

SOUPS AND SALADS

SOUPS AND SALADS

Creamy Artichoke Soup

This soup is easy to prepare in advance. Reheat just before serving.

2	(14-ounce) cans artichoke hearts, drained
1	tablespoon butter
6	green onion bulbs, chopped
3	tablespoons minced fresh parsley
2	garlic cloves, minced
¼	cup plus 2 tablespoons flour
2	cups 2% milk
2	(14-ounce) cans chicken broth
	salt to taste
	white pepper to taste
2	teaspoons grated Parmesan cheese (optional)
½	teaspoon nutmeg

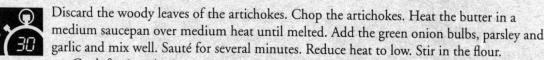 Discard the woody leaves of the artichokes. Chop the artichokes. Heat the butter in a medium saucepan over medium heat until melted. Add the green onion bulbs, parsley and garlic and mix well. Sauté for several minutes. Reduce heat to low. Stir in the flour.

Cook for 3 to 4 minutes, stirring constantly; do not allow the flour to brown. Add the 2% milk and broth alternately, stirring constantly. Stir in the artichokes. Season with salt and white pepper. Add the cheese and nutmeg and mix well.

Pour the soup into a blender or food processor container. Process until puréed. Return the soup to the saucepan. Cook just until heated through, stirring frequently. Ladle into soup bowls.

YIELD: 6 (1½-CUP) SERVINGS

Nutrients Per Serving: **Cal 190; Prot 13 g; Carbo 26 g; T Fat 5 g; (Saturated Fat 3 g); Chol 13 mg; Fiber 8 g; Sod 977 mg**

Snowy Weekend Cassoulet

On a cold day, this soup will fill your home with a wonderful smell. Double the recipe and freeze for future use.

¼	cup dried lentils
¼	cup dried split peas
2	quarts water
1	(28-ounce) can diced tomatoes
1	(15-ounce) can black beans, drained, rinsed
1	(15-ounce) can Great Northern beans, drained, rinsed
¼	cup barley
1	medium onion, chopped
2	ribs celery, chopped
½	large green bell pepper, chopped
2	garlic cloves, minced
¼	teaspoon thyme
	red pepper to taste
2	boneless skinless chicken breast halves, cubed
7	ounces smoked reduced-fat sausage, sliced
1	cup chopped lean ham

Sort and rinse the lentils and split peas. Combine with the water, undrained tomatoes, beans, barley, onion, celery, green pepper, garlic, thyme and red pepper in a stockpot and mix well. Simmer for 1 hour, stirring occasionally.

Pre-cook the chicken breasts to 170 degrees, then cube and add with the sausage and ham. Simmer until heated through, stirring occasionally. Ladle into soup bowls.

YIELD: 8 SERVINGS

Nutrients Per Serving: Cal 308; Prot 32 g; Carbo 37 g; T Fat 4 g; (Saturated Fat 1 g); Chol 51 mg; Fiber 11 g; Sod 727 mg

*G*rate additional fresh vegetables when they are plentiful in the grocery or garden and store in recipe-size portions in sealable freezer bags or freezer containers. The vegetables will be ready for adding to sauces and soups, and even to muffins, breads, and desserts. An easy way to incorporate Five-A-Day.

Tasty Turkey Chili

1¼   pounds ground turkey
¼   cup water
2   cups chopped onions
2   large garlic cloves, minced
1   (15-ounce) can tomato sauce
1   (14-ounce) can peeled whole no-salt-added tomatoes, chopped
1   tablespoon chili powder
1   bay leaf
1   teaspoon cumin
½   teaspoon sugar
1   (15-ounce) can pinto beans, drained
1   cup frozen whole kernel corn
   salt and pepper to taste
1   cup shredded reduced-fat Cheddar cheese (optional)

Brown the ground turkey with the water in a 3-quart saucepan, stirring until the ground turkey is crumbly. Add the onions and garlic and mix well. Cook for 5 minutes or until the onions are tender, stirring frequently. Add additional water if needed. Stir in the tomato sauce, undrained tomatoes, chili powder, bay leaf, cumin and sugar.

    Simmer, covered, for 20 minutes, stirring occasionally. Add the beans, corn, salt and pepper and mix well. Simmer for 10 minutes longer, stirring occasionally. Discard the bay leaf. Ladle into chili bowls. Sprinkle with the cheese.

YIELD: 6 SERVINGS

Nutrients Per Serving: **Cal 304; Prot 25 g; Carbo 31 g; T Fat 10 g; (Saturated Fat 3 g); Chol 68 mg; Fiber 7 g; Sod 731 mg**

Hearty White Chili

A new version of an old favorite that is sure to please traditional chili fans.

1	pound boneless skinless chicken breasts
1	medium yellow onion, chopped
1	tablespoon olive oil
1	(4-ounce) can green chiles, drained, chopped
3	garlic cloves, minced
1	teaspoon cumin
3/4	teaspoon oregano
1/8	teaspoon cayenne pepper
1	(16-ounce) can cannellini beans, drained, rinsed
2	(16-ounce) cans reduced-sodium chicken broth
1/2	cup shredded Monterey Jack cheese

Cut the chicken into bite-size pieces. Sauté the chicken and onion in the olive oil in a large saucepan until the chicken is white and the onion is tender. Stir in the chiles, garlic, cumin, oregano and cayenne pepper. Sauté for 2 minutes. Add the beans and broth and mix well.

Bring to a boil; reduce heat. Simmer for 45 to 60 minutes or until of the desired consistency, stirring occasionally. Ladle into chili bowls. Sprinkle with the cheese.

YIELD: 6 SERVINGS

Nutrients Per Serving: Cal 232; Prot 23 g; Carbo 15 g; T Fat 8 g; (Saturated Fat 3 g); Chol 53 mg; Fiber 4 g; Sod 553 mg

Cheddar Chicken Chowder

This delicious chowder is hearty enough to be an entrée.

1	pound boneless skinless chicken breasts
1	cup chopped onion
1	cup chopped red bell pepper
2	garlic cloves, minced
2	teaspoons olive oil
4½	cups fat-free chicken broth
1¾	cups chopped red potatoes
2¼	cups frozen whole kernel corn
2	cups skim milk
½	cup flour
¾	cup shredded reduced-fat sharp Cheddar cheese (3 ounces)
½	teaspoon salt
¼	teaspoon pepper

Cut the chicken into bite-size pieces. Sauté the chicken, onion, red pepper and garlic in the olive oil in a large skillet for 5 minutes. Stir in the broth and red potatoes. Bring to a boil; reduce heat. Simmer, covered, for 20 minutes or until the potatoes are tender, stirring occasionally. Add the corn and mix well.

Whisk the skim milk into the flour in a bowl until blended. Add to the chicken mixture gradually, whisking constantly. Cook over medium heat for 15 minutes or until thickened, stirring frequently. Stir in the cheese, salt and pepper. Ladle into soup bowls.

YIELD: 7 SERVINGS

Nutrients Per Serving: Cal 279; Prot 26 g; Carbo 32 g; T Fat 6 g; (Saturated Fat 2 g); Chol 44 mg; Fiber 3 g; Sod 533 mg

Greek Lemon Chicken Soup

This delightful lemon soup has a creamy yellow appearance. Serve for lunch or as a first course with Pork Souvlaki Kabobs on page 89.

3   cups chicken broth

⅓   cup orzo

⅓   cup finely chopped cooked chicken

3   tablespoons fresh lemon juice

1   egg, beaten

Bring the broth to a boil in a saucepan. Stir in the orzo and chicken. Simmer for 11 minutes or until the orzo is tender, stirring occasionally. Stir in the lemon juice. Bring to a boil.

Remove from heat. Add the egg gradually, whisking constantly. Ladle into soup bowls. Do not reheat. Serve immediately.

YIELD: 4 SERVINGS

Nutrients Per Serving: Cal 125; Prot 10 g; Carbo 12 g; T Fat 3 g; (Saturated Fat 1 g); Chol 64 mg; Fiber <1 g; Sod 609 mg

Southwestern Chicken Soup

Lunch doesn't get any easier!

3   boneless skinless chicken breast halves
8   cups chicken broth
2   (15-ounce) cans kidney beans, drained, rinsed
1   (16-ounce) package frozen whole kernel corn
2   cups salsa
1   cup uncooked instant rice

 Cut the chicken into bite-size pieces. Combine the chicken, broth, beans, corn and salsa in a stockpot and mix well. Bring to a boil; reduce heat. Simmer for 20 minutes or until the chicken is cooked through, stirring occasionally. Remove from heat. Stir in the rice. Let stand, covered, for 5 minutes. Ladle into soup bowls.

YIELD: 8 SERVINGS

Nutrients Per Serving: Cal 345; Prot 34 g; Carbo 43 g; T Fat 5 g; (Saturated Fat 1 g); Chol 55 mg; Fiber 6 g; Sod 1476 mg

Autumn Curry Soup

The seasonings give this soup an appealing sweetness, and the use of canned pumpkin makes the preparation quick.

1	tablespoon vegetable oil
⅓	cup chopped onion
1	garlic clove, crushed
1	teaspoon curry powder
¼	teaspoon coriander
3	cups chicken broth
2	cups canned pumpkin
	salt and pepper to taste

Heat the oil in a saucepan until hot. Add the onion and garlic. Sauté until the onion is tender. Stir in the curry powder and coriander. Cook for 1 minute, stirring frequently. Stir in the broth and pumpkin. Bring to a boil, stirring occasionally.

Pour the pumpkin mixture into a blender or food processor container. Process until puréed. Season with salt and pepper. Ladle into soup bowls. Serve immediately. May substitute cooked butternut squash for the pumpkin for variety.

YIELD: 6 SERVINGS

Nutrients Per Serving: **Cal 71; Prot 4 g; Carbo 8 g; T Fat 3 g; (Saturated Fat <1 g); Chol 0 mg; Fiber 4 g; Sod 392 mg**

Creamy Curry Onion Soup

1	tablespoon butter
4	cups sliced onions
1	tablespoon curry powder
8	cups chicken broth
½	cup uncooked rice
	reduced-fat or fat-free sour cream (optional)

Heat the butter in a 3-quart stockpot until melted. Add the onions. Sauté for 5 to 10 minutes or until tender. Stir in the curry powder. Sauté for 5 minutes longer. Add the broth and rice and mix well.

Bring to a boil; reduce heat. Simmer, covered, for 20 to 30 minutes or until the rice is tender, stirring occasionally. Reserve 1 cup of the soup.

Pour the remaining soup into a blender or food processor container. Process until smooth. Stir in the reserved soup. Serve immediately or reheat in stockpot if desired. Ladle into soup bowls. Top each serving with a dollop of sour cream.

YIELD: 8 (1-CUP) SERVINGS

Nutrients Per Serving: Cal 127; Prot 7 g; Carbo 18 g; T Fat 3 g; (Saturated Fat 1 g); Chol 4 mg; Fiber 2 g; Sod 794 mg

Hot and Sour Soup

This soup makes a fabulous first course or entrée.

1	boneless skinless chicken breast half
2	tablespoons white wine
8	cups chicken broth
1	(8-ounce) can mushrooms, drained, chopped
1	(8-ounce) can bamboo shoots, drained, julienned
⅓	cup white vinegar
2	tablespoons reduced-sodium soy sauce
½	cup water
¼	cup cornstarch
1	pound firm tofu, cut into ½-inch strips
2	teaspoons sesame oil
1½	teaspoons white pepper
2	eggs, beaten
	crushed red pepper to taste (optional)

 Cut the chicken into thin strips. Combine the chicken and white wine in a sealable plastic bag and seal tightly. Toss to coat. Marinate at room temperature for 10 minutes. Bring the broth to a boil in a stockpot. Add the chicken mixture, mushrooms and bamboo shoots; reduce heat.

Simmer for 5 minutes, stirring occasionally. Stir in the vinegar and soy sauce. Combine the water and cornstarch in a bowl, stirring until smooth. Add to the broth mixture and mix well.

Cook until thickened, stirring constantly. Add the tofu and mix well. Remove from heat. Stir in the sesame oil and white pepper. Add the eggs gradually, stirring constantly. Add the red pepper for a spicier soup. Ladle into soup bowls.

YIELD: 10 SERVINGS

Nutrients Per Serving: Cal 163; Prot 15 g; Carbo 14 g; T Fat 5 g; (Saturated Fat 1 g); Chol 57 mg; Fiber 1 g; Sod 868 mg

Spicy African Rice and Peanut Stew

A definite crowd pleaser made from a unique combination of ingredients.

1	tablespoon canola oil
1	large onion, chopped
1	medium sweet potato, peeled, diced
2	garlic cloves, minced
8	cups reduced-sodium chicken broth
1	cup uncooked white rice
1	teaspoon thyme
½	teaspoon cumin
3	cups salsa
3	(16-ounce) cans garbanzo beans, drained, rinsed
1	small zucchini, cut into ¼-inch slices
⅔	cup creamy or chunky peanut butter

Heat the canola oil in a stockpot until hot. Add the onion, sweet potato and garlic. Sauté until the onion is tender. Stir in the broth, rice, thyme and cumin. Bring to a boil; reduce heat.

Simmer for 20 minutes or until the rice and vegetables are tender, stirring frequently. Add the salsa, beans and zucchini and mix well. Simmer for 15 minutes or until the zucchini is tender, stirring occasionally. Stir in the peanut butter. Ladle into soup bowls. Serve with rolls or crusty French bread.

YIELD: 16 SERVINGS

Nutrients Per Serving: Cal 258; Prot 10 g; Carbo 38 g; T Fat 8 g; (Saturated Fat 2 g); Chol 2 mg; Fiber 6 g; Sod 571 mg

Tomatoes and tomato products are rich in antioxidant vitamins A and C, as well as lycopene, a phytochemical that gives them their red color and is believed to function as a potent antioxidant.

A review of over seventy studies on tomatoes and such tomato products as soups, sauces, and juices, indicates that tomatoes show promise in substantially decreasing the risk for developing a variety of cancers.

Mexican Tomato Soup with Lime

A fun and enticing version of tomato soup.

1½	teaspoons canola oil
3	garlic cloves, minced
2	teaspoons cumin
1	(46-ounce) can tomato juice
2	cups chopped fresh tomatoes
¼	cup fresh lime juice
1	teaspoon basil
	hot pepper sauce to taste
1	ounce reduced-fat tortilla chips (about 20)

Heat the canola oil in a large saucepan over low heat. Add the garlic and cumin. Cook for 1 minute, stirring constantly; do not brown. Stir in the tomato juice, tomatoes, lime juice, basil and hot pepper sauce.
Simmer for 10 minutes, stirring occasionally. Crush the tortilla chips into 6 soup bowls. Ladle the soup over the tortilla chips.

YIELD: 6 SERVINGS

Nutrients Per Serving: Cal 83; Prot 3 g; Carbo 17 g; T Fat 2 g; (Saturated Fat <1 g); Chol 0 mg; Fiber 2 g; Sod 817 mg

Wild Rice and Chicken Soup

1   (6-ounce) package long grain and wild rice
½   teaspoon salt
2   tablespoons margarine
2   boneless skinless chicken breast halves, cut into ½-inch pieces
1   tablespoon minced onion
½   cup flour
3   cups chicken broth
½   cup shredded carrot
1   (12-ounce) can evaporated skim milk
2   tablespoons white cooking wine
    chopped fresh parsley to taste

Cook the rice using package directions, adding ½ teaspoon salt to the cooking water and omitting the margarine and seasoning packet. Heat the margarine in a large saucepan until melted. Add the chicken and onion and mix well. Sauté until the onion is tender and the chicken is cooked through. Add the flour, stirring until mixed. Stir in the broth.

Bring to a boil, stirring constantly. Stir in the carrot. Boil for 1 minute, stirring constantly. Add 2 cups of the rice and mix well. Simmer for 5 minutes, stirring occasionally. Add the evaporated milk and cooking wine and mix well. Cook just until heated through, stirring occasionally. Ladle into soup bowls. Sprinkle with parsley.

Tip: Freeze the leftover rice for future use in soups and casseroles. This will save preparation time later.

YIELD: 4 SERVINGS

Nutrients Per Serving: Cal 442; Prot 42 g; Carbo 42 g; T Fat 10 g; (Saturated Fat 2 g); Chol 76 mg; Fiber 2 g; Sod 1153 mg

Seafood Chowder

1	large onion, chopped
1	large green bell pepper, chopped
2	large ribs celery, chopped
2	garlic cloves, minced
1	tablespoon olive oil
2	(14-ounce) cans chopped tomatoes
2	(8-ounce) cans tomato sauce
1	cup white wine
2	tablespoons parsley flakes
1	teaspoon basil
½	teaspoon oregano
1	bay leaf
1	pound crab meat, flaked
1	pound whitefish, cubed
	cayenne pepper to taste

Sauté the onion, green pepper, celery and garlic in the olive oil in a medium stockpot until the vegetables are tender. Add the undrained tomatoes, tomato sauce, wine, parsley flakes, basil, oregano and bay leaf and mix well.

Cook for 20 to 30 minutes, stirring occasionally. Stir in the crab meat and whitefish. Cook for 10 minutes longer or until the fish is cooked through, stirring occasionally. Stir in cayenne pepper. Discard the bay leaf. Ladle over hot cooked rice in soup bowls.

YIELD: 8 SERVINGS

Nutrients Per Serving: **Cal 224; Prot 25 g; Carbo 12 g; T Fat 6 g; (Saturated Fat 1 g); Chol 75 mg; Fiber 3 g; Sod 756 mg**

Do not store uncooked fish in the refrigerator for more than twenty-four hours. Uncooked poultry or ground beef can be stored in the refrigerator for one to two days and uncooked meat for three to five days.

Vegetable Lentil Soup

¾   cup dried lentils

4   (14-ounce) cans vegetable broth

2   cups sliced mushrooms

1   cup chopped onion

1   cup chopped celery

1   cup chopped unpeeled potato

½   cup chopped carrot

½   cup frozen green beans

½   cup chopped red bell pepper

½   cup pearl barley

1   tablespoon cumin

    salt and pepper to taste

1   (14-ounce) can diced tomatoes

1   (14-ounce) can vegetable broth (optional)

Sort and rinse the lentils. Combine the lentils, 4 cans broth, mushrooms, onion, celery, potato, carrot, green beans, red pepper, barley, cumin, salt and pepper in a stockpot and mix well. Bring to a simmer over medium heat, stirring occasionally. Reduce heat to low.

Simmer, covered, for 30 minutes, stirring occasionally. Stir in the undrained tomatoes. Simmer for 15 minutes longer, stirring occasionally. Add 1 can broth if needed for a thinner consistency and mix well. Simmer just until heated through, stirring occasionally. Ladle into soup bowls.

Tip: To save preparation time, substitute frozen vegetables for the fresh vegetables.

YIELD: 6 SERVINGS

Nutrients Per Serving: Cal 224; Prot 12 g; Carbo 44 g; T Fat 2 g; (Saturated Fat <1 g); Chol 0 mg; Fiber 11 g; Sod 1268 mg

Creamy Fruit and Nut Medley

2 (11-ounce) cans mandarin oranges, drained
1 (20-ounce) can juice-pack pineapple tidbits, drained
2 apples, chopped
2 bananas, sliced
1 cup grated carrot
½ cup raisins
¼ cup chopped pecans
¾ cup orange fat-free yogurt
1 tablespoon honey
½ teaspoon cinnamon

Combine the mandarin oranges, pineapple, apples, bananas, carrot, raisins and pecans in a bowl and mix gently.
    Mix the yogurt, honey and cinnamon in a bowl. Add to the fruit mixture and toss gently to coat. Chill, covered, until serving time.

YIELD: 8 SERVINGS

Nutrients Per Serving: **Cal 224; Prot 3 g; Carbo 51 g; T Fat 3 g; (Saturated Fat <1 g); Chol <1 mg; Fiber 4 g; Sod 27 mg**

Pineapple juice, like lemon and citrus juice, keeps sliced apples, pears, and bananas from turning brown. When making a fresh fruit salad, add a can of pineapple chunks with the juice to eliminate the tart lemon taste and add variety.

Marinated Beet Salad

2   pounds fresh beets, boiled, peeled, thinly sliced
¼   large red onion, thinly sliced
2   tablespoons each reduced-sodium soy sauce and red wine vinegar
1   teaspoon each freshly grated gingerroot and grated orange zest
¼   teaspoon pepper

Layer the beets and red onion in a serving bowl. Whisk the soy sauce, wine vinegar, gingerroot, orange zest and pepper in a bowl until mixed. Pour over the prepared layers. Chill, covered, for 1 hour or longer. Stir gently before serving.

YIELD: 6 SERVINGS

Nutrients Per Serving: Cal 71; Prot 3 g; Carbo 15 g; T Fat <1 g; (Saturated Fat <1 g); Chol 0 mg; Fiber 3 g; Sod 276 mg

Curry Broccoli Potato Salad

3   cups ½-inch pieces unpeeled red potatoes
2   tablespoons water
1   teaspoon salt
2   cups fresh small broccoli florets
¼   cup plain fat-free yogurt
3   tablespoons reduced-fat mayonnaise
¼   cup minced purple onion
¼   teaspoon each sugar and curry powder
⅛   teaspoon white pepper

Combine the red potatoes, water and ½ teaspoon of the salt in a microwave-safe dish. Microwave, covered, on High for 7 to 9 minutes, stirring at 3-minute intervals. Stir in the broccoli. Microwave on High for 2 to 2½ minutes or until the broccoli is tender. Let stand for 5 minutes; drain.

Mix the yogurt, mayonnaise, onion, remaining ½ teaspoon salt, sugar, curry powder and white pepper in a bowl. Add to broccoli mixture; toss gently to coat. Chill, covered, until serving time.

YIELD: 6 SERVINGS

Nutrients Per Serving: Cal 101; Prot 3 g; Carbo 18 g; T Fat 3 g; (Saturated Fat <1 g); Chol 3 mg; Fiber 2 g; Sod 457 mg

Steak and Roasted Vegetable Salad

1	medium zucchini, cut into 1-inch slices
1	medium eggplant, cut into 1-inch slices
1	large red or green bell pepper, cut into 1-inch strips
1	medium onion, cut into 1-inch wedges
16	small mushrooms
¾	cup fat-free Italian salad dressing
2	tablespoons balsamic vinegar
2	garlic cloves, crushed
1	teaspoon rosemary
¼	teaspoon pepper
1	pound (1-inch thick) beef top loin
¼	teaspoon salt
8	cups torn lettuce

Spray a 10x15-inch pan lightly with nonstick cooking spray. Arrange the zucchini, eggplant, red pepper, onion and mushrooms in the pan. Spray the vegetables generously with nonstick cooking spray.

Whisk the salad dressing, balsamic vinegar, garlic, rosemary and pepper in a bowl. Drizzle over the vegetables. Roast at 425 degrees for 30 to 35 minutes or until the vegetables are tender, stirring once.

Heat a large nonstick skillet over medium heat. Add the beef. Cook for 12 to 15 minutes for medium-rare to medium, turning once. Let stand for 10 minutes. Sprinkle with the salt. Trim the fat from the beef. Slice against the grain into thin strips.

Arrange equals amount of the lettuce on each of 4 dinner plates. Arrange the beef and roasted vegetables over the lettuce. Serve immediately.

YIELD: 4 SERVINGS

Nutrients Per Serving: Cal 274; Prot 31 g; Carbo 23 g; T Fat 7 g; (Saturated Fat 2 g); Chol 75 mg; Fiber 7 g; Sod 655 mg

Make your eggplant sweat. Sweating can pull moisture out of an eggplant. This is especially beneficial when the eggplant is to be fried, since the sweating process keeps it from absorbing as much oil. This process can also take out some of the bitter taste of eggplant that have been stored too long. To sweat, sprinkle the eggplant slices or cubes lightly with salt and place in a colander. →

Raspberry Chicken Salad

Beautiful to look at and tastes even better.

4   boneless skinless chicken breast halves
⅓   cup raspberry preserves
⅓   cup frozen orange juice concentrate
⅓   cup reduced-sodium soy sauce
2   tablespoons rice vinegar
½   teaspoon chili powder
½   teaspoon garlic powder
6   cups mixed salad greens
⅓   cup fat-free raspberry vinaigrette
½   cup fresh raspberries

Place the chicken in a sealable plastic bag. Combine the preserves, orange juice concentrate, soy sauce, rice vinegar, chili powder and garlic powder in a bowl and mix well. Pour over the chicken and seal tightly. Toss to coat. Marinate in the refrigerator for 2 hours or longer, turning occasionally.

Grill the chicken over hot coals for 5 to 6 minutes per side or until thermometer placed in center of breast measures 170 degrees. Cut into ½-inch strips.

Toss the salad greens with the vinaigrette in a bowl. Arrange an equal amount of the salad greens on each of 4 dinner plates. Top with the chicken. Sprinkle with the raspberries.

YIELD: 4 SERVINGS

Nutrients Per Serving: Cal 457; Prot 57 g; Carbo 39 g; T Fat 7 g; (Saturated Fat 2 g); Chol 146 mg; Fiber 3 g; Sod 862 mg
Nutritional information includes the entire amount of marinade.

Let stand for one hour or longer. Blot the juices that come to the surface with paper towels. Rinse the eggplant and pat dry. You may want to reduce the amount of salt used in your eggplant dishes because of the salt added during the sweating process.

Imperial Krab Salad

1	pound imitation crab meat
1	cup sliced celery
4	green onions, chopped
¼	cup reduced-fat mayonnaise
¼	cup skim milk
1	tablespoon lemon juice
1	teaspoon dillweed
½	teaspoon pepper
	hot pepper sauce to taste
4	tomatoes, cut into wedges

Flake the crab meat into a bowl. Stir in the celery and green onions. Combine the mayonnaise, skim milk, lemon juice, dillweed, pepper and hot pepper sauce in a bowl and mix well. Add to the crab meat mixture and mix gently.

Chill, covered, for several hours. Serve surrounded with tomato wedges.

Tip: Imitation crab meat is made from mild-flavor fish to which crab flavoring has been added. It has a distinctive crab taste without the high price.

YIELD: 4 SERVINGS

Nutrients Per Serving: Cal 215; Prot 17 g; Carbo 24 g; T Fat 6 g; (Saturated Fat 1 g); Chol 60 mg; Fiber 2 g; Sod 1111 mg

Dilled Shrimp and Rice

This light salad is perfect for a summer evening.

1	cup white rice
¼	cup white wine vinegar
2	tablespoons canola oil
1	tablespoon chopped fresh dillweed, or 2 teaspoons dried dillweed
½	teaspoon salt
¼	teaspoon pepper
8	ounces snow peas
8	ounces medium shrimp, steamed, peeled, deveined
¼	cup chopped green onions
	juice of ½ lemon

Cook the rice using package directions. Combine the wine vinegar, canola oil, dillweed, salt and pepper in a jar with a tight-fitting lid and shake to mix. Pour 2 tablespoons of the dressing over the hot rice in a bowl and toss gently. Chill, covered, for 1 hour or longer.

Steam the snow peas in a steamer until tender; drain. Combine the rice, shrimp, green onions and remaining dressing in a bowl and mix well.

Mound the rice mixture on a large serving platter or on individual dinner plates. Arrange the snow peas spoke fashion around the outer edge of the rice. Drizzle with the lemon juice just before serving. Garnish with additional dillweed and/or additional green onions.

YIELD: 4 SERVINGS

Nutrients Per Serving: Cal 312; Prot 13 g; Carbo 46 g; T Fat 8 g; (Saturated Fat 1 g); Chol 67 mg; Fiber 2 g; Sod 374 mg

Cruciferous is the term for a large family of vegetables including broccoli, cauliflower, cabbage, brussels sprouts, turnips, rutabaga, radishes, kale, and bok choy. These vegetables can easily be identified by their strong aromas, but what makes them so special is their potential cancer-fighting properties. Some studies suggest that they may be especially helpful in protecting against colon and rectal cancers.

Tuna Summer Salad

2	(6-ounce) cans water-pack tuna, drained
1	cup chopped green cabbage
½	cup chopped red bell pepper
2	tablespoons reduced-fat mayonnaise
2	tablespoons plain fat-free yogurt
½	teaspoon dillweed
¼	teaspoon pepper
4	large lettuce leaves

Toss the tuna, cabbage and red pepper in a bowl. Combine the mayonnaise, yogurt, dillweed and pepper in a bowl and mix well. Add to the tuna mixture and mix well.

Arrange 1 lettuce leaf on each of 4 plates. Spoon the tuna mixture on top of the lettuce.

Tip: The tuna salad may be prepared 1 day in advance and stored, covered, in the refrigerator.

YIELD: 4 SERVINGS

Nutrients Per Serving: Cal 133; Prot 22 g; Carbo 4 g; T Fat 3 g; (Saturated Fat <1 g); Chol 27 mg; Fiber 1 g; Sod 340 mg

Spicy Black Bean Salsa Salad

This easy main dish salad requires no cooking. Serve leftovers as a dip with baked tortilla chips.

2	(14-ounce) cans black beans, drained, rinsed
1	(14-ounce) can garbanzo beans, drained, rinsed
1	cup frozen whole kernel corn, thawed
½	cup chopped fresh cilantro
½	cup sliced green onions
¼	cup chopped red onion
¼	cup lime juice
1	tablespoon hot pepper sauce
1	tablespoon canola oil
2	garlic cloves, minced
1	large tomato, chopped
4	cups shredded lettuce
	baked tortilla chips (optional)

Combine the beans, corn, cilantro, green onions and red onion in a bowl and mix gently. Whisk the lime juice, hot pepper sauce, canola oil and garlic in a bowl. Pour over the bean mixture, tossing gently to coat. Chill, covered, for 2 to 10 hours.

Stir in the tomato just before serving. Arrange ½ cup of the shredded lettuce on each of 8 salad plates. Top with the black bean salad. Sprinkle with tortilla chips.

YIELD: 8 SERVINGS

Nutrients Per Serving: Cal 184; Prot 9 g; Carbo 32 g; T Fat 3 g;
(Saturated Fat <1 g); Chol 0 mg; Fiber 9 g; Sod 507 mg

Parmesan Pasta and Bean Salad

12   ounces rotini
¾   cup plain fat-free yogurt
¾   cup reduced-fat or fat-free mayonnaise
1½   tablespoons Dijon mustard
6   tablespoons grated Parmesan cheese
1½   teaspoons dillweed
       pepper to taste
1   (15-ounce) can kidneys beans, drained, rinsed
1   large red bell pepper, roasted, chopped
¾   cup chopped tomato
½   cup chopped celery
2   carrots, coarsely shredded or chopped
2   tablespoons chopped fresh parsley

Cook the pasta using package directions. Drain and rinse with cold water. Combine the yogurt, mayonnaise, Dijon mustard, cheese, dillweed and pepper in a bowl and mix well.

Combine the pasta, beans, red pepper, tomato, celery, carrots and parsley in a bowl and mix gently. Add the yogurt mixture, tossing gently to coat. Chill, covered, until serving time.

YIELD: 10 SERVINGS

Nutrients Per Serving: Cal 240; Prot 9 g; Carbo 35 g; T Fat 8 g;
(Saturated Fat 1 g); Chol 9 mg; Fiber 4 g; Sod 423 mg

Asiago Pasta Salad

3   cups boiling water
4   ounces sun-dried tomatoes
12 ounces pesto-flavor rotini or other shaped pasta
2   tablespoons olive oil
⅛   teaspoon ground pepper
2   garlic cloves, crushed
10 ounces fresh spinach, trimmed, torn
¾   cup grated asiago cheese (3 ounces)
¼   cup finely grated fresh Parmesan cheese (1 ounce)

Pour the boiling water over the sun-dried tomatoes in a bowl. Let stand for 10 minutes. Drain and chop.
    Cook the pasta using package directions; drain.
    Combine the sun-dried tomatoes, olive oil, pepper and garlic in a bowl and mix well. Add the pasta and spinach and toss gently. Sprinkle with the asiago cheese and Parmesan cheese and toss gently.

YIELD: 8 SERVINGS

Nutrients Per Serving: Cal 275; Prot 12 g; Carbo 38 g; T Fat 8 g; (Saturated Fat 3 g); Chol 12 mg; Fiber 4 g; Sod 128 mg

Hard cheeses, such as Parmesan, Romano, and asiago, typically have a strong distinctive flavor. Because of this robust flavor, you can use a smaller amount in recipes and thus cut back on fat grams. Asiago cheese is described as having a robust, slightly nutty flavor. Look for it in the "specialty" or imported-cheese section of your local grocery store.

Crunchy Pea and Cashew Salad

Great for picnics! Serve with Baked Sour Cream Chicken on page 98 and Low-Fat Brownies on page 203 next time you go to Red Rocks for a concert.

1	(10-ounce) package frozen green peas, thawed
1	cup cauliflowerets
1	cup chopped celery
⅓	cup cashews
¼	cup sliced green onions
½	cup fat-free ranch salad dressing
¼	cup reduced-fat sour cream
½	teaspoon dillweed

Combine the peas, cauliflower, celery, cashews and green onions in a bowl and mix well. Mix the salad dressing, sour cream and dillweed in a bowl. Add to the vegetable mixture, tossing to coat. Chill, covered, until serving time.

YIELD: 8 SERVINGS

Nutrients Per Serving: Cal 100; Prot 4 g; Carbo 14 g; T Fat 3 g; (Saturated Fat 1 g); Chol 3 mg; Fiber 3 g; Sod 218 mg

San Juan Salad with Creamy Tofu Dressing

Tofu gives this reduced-fat dressing a rich creamy texture.

CREAMY TOFU DRESSING

¼	cup soft tofu
1	tablespoon cider vinegar
1	teaspoon honey
1	garlic clove, minced
¼	teaspoon Dijon mustard
¼	teaspoon celery salt
	pepper to taste

SALAD

1	(15-ounce) can small white beans, drained, rinsed
1	cup chopped zucchini
½	cup chopped tomato
6	basil leaves, julienned
2	cups torn spinach

For the dressing, combine the tofu, vinegar, honey, garlic, Dijon mustard, celery salt and pepper in a blender or food processor container. Process until smooth.

For the salad, combine the beans, zucchini, tomato and basil in a bowl and mix gently. Add the dressing, tossing to coat. Arrange the spinach on a serving platter. Mound the bean mixture over the spinach. Serve immediately.

YIELD: 4 SERVINGS

Nutrients Per Serving: Cal 153; Prot 10 g; Carbo 28 g; T Fat 1 g; (Saturated Fat <1 g); Chol 0 mg; Fiber 6 g; Sod 122 mg

Strawberry Spinach Salad

An attractive addition to any meal.

POPPY SEED DRESSING

⅓	cup sugar
¼	cup cider vinegar
2	tablespoons canola oil
1	tablespoon poppy seeds
¼	teaspoon paprika
¼	teaspoon Worcestershire sauce

SALAD

1	pint strawberries, cut into quarters
10	ounces fresh spinach, trimmed, torn

For the dressing, combine the sugar, vinegar and canola oil in a saucepan. Cook over low heat until the sugar dissolves, stirring frequently. Cool slightly. Stir in the poppy seeds, paprika and Worcestershire sauce.

For the salad, mix the strawberries and spinach in a salad bowl. Add the dressing, tossing gently to coat. Serve immediately.

Tip: To remove grit from fresh spinach and assorted greens, rinse in a mixture of 6 to 8 quarts water and 2 tablespoons vinegar. Rinse again in fresh water.

YIELD: 6 SERVINGS

Nutrients Per Serving: Cal 114; Prot 2 g; Carbo 17 g; T Fat 5 g;
(Saturated Fat <1 g); Chol 0 mg; Fiber 2 g; Sod 30 mg

Spinach Potluck Salad

Most of these ingredients can be purchased at the grocery store on your way to the potluck...but make the dressing at home.

SPINACH SALAD DRESSING

⅓	cup canola oil
¼	cup rice vinegar
¼	cup catsup
2	tablespoons sugar
⅛	teaspoon pepper

SALAD

10	ounces fresh spinach, trimmed, torn
10	ounces mixed salad greens
2	cups bean sprouts
1	(4-ounce) can water chestnuts, drained, sliced
2	hard-cooked eggs, chopped
¼	cup crumbled crisp-fried bacon

 For the dressing, combine the canola oil, rice vinegar, catsup, sugar and pepper in a jar with a tight-fitting lid and seal tightly. Shake to mix.

For the salad, toss the spinach, salad greens, bean sprouts, water chestnuts, eggs and bacon in a salad bowl. Drizzle with the dressing just before serving.

YIELD: 10 SERVINGS

Nutrients Per Serving: Cal 122; Prot 3 g; Carbo 9 g; T Fat 9 g; (Saturated Fat 1 g); Chol 43 mg; Fiber 2 g; Sod 129 mg

Return any leftover cold foods to the refrigerator as soon as possible. When traveling with cold foods, store in an insulated container or with a reusable freezer gel pack or frozen box of juice.

Mixed Greens with Herbed Merlot Dressing

HERBED MERLOT DRESSING

¼	cup Merlot or Cabernet Sauvignon
1	tablespoon olive oil
1	tablespoon chopped fresh basil
1	tablespoon chopped fresh oregano
1	teaspoon minced fresh garlic

SALAD

2	tablespoons pine nuts
4	cups mixed salad greens
¼	cup crumbled Gorgonzola cheese

For the dressing, whisk the wine, olive oil, basil, oregano and garlic in a bowl until mixed.

For the salad, toast the pine nuts in a small skillet over medium heat for 5 minutes or until light brown, stirring frequently. Let stand until cool. Arrange 1 cup of the salad greens in each of 4 salad bowls. Top each salad with 1 tablespoon Gorgonzola cheese, 1½ teaspoons pine nuts and 1 tablespoon of the dressing.

Tip: May substitute 2 teaspoons dried basil for the fresh basil and 2 teaspoons dried oregano for the fresh oregano.

YIELD: 4 SERVINGS

Nutrients Per Serving: Cal 102; Prot 4 g; Carbo 3 g; T Fat 8 g; (Saturated Fat 2 g); Chol 6 mg; Fiber 1 g; Sod 113 mg

*P*ackaged fresh-cut salad mixes are a great time-saver and offer a variety of salad greens. However, do not just throw them in a bowl and serve. Place the greens in a colander and rinse well with cold water before serving.

Mixed Greens with Pears, Bleu Cheese and Pecans

DIJON DRESSING

2	tablespoons chicken broth
2	tablespoons white wine vinegar
1	garlic clove, minced
1	tablespoon olive oil
1	teaspoon Dijon mustard
1	teaspoon Worcestershire sauce
½	teaspoon sugar
¼	teaspoon pepper

SALAD

¼	cup pecans
6	cups mixed salad greens
2	pears, peeled, sliced
1	ounce bleu cheese, crumbled

For the dressing, whisk the broth, wine vinegar, garlic, olive oil, Dijon mustard, Worcestershire sauce, sugar and pepper in a bowl until the sugar dissolves.

For the salad, spread the pecans on a baking sheet. Toast at 350 degrees for 5 minutes or until light brown and fragrant. Let stand until cool. Toss the salad greens with the dressing in a bowl. Divide evenly among 4 salad plates. Arrange the sliced pears around the edge of each salad. Sprinkle with the cheese and pecans.

YIELD: 4 SERVINGS

Nutrients Per Serving: Cal 173; Prot 4 g; Carbo 18 g; T Fat 11 g; (Saturated Fat 2 g); Chol 5 mg; Fiber 4 g; Sod 190 mg

Garlic Caesar Salad

CAESAR DRESSING

3	tablespoons white wine vinegar
2	tablespoons freshly grated Parmesan cheese
1½	tablespoons olive oil
1	tablespoon minced onion
3	garlic cloves, minced
2	teaspoons capers
1	teaspoon Dijon mustard
	salt and pepper to taste

FRENCH BREAD CROUTONS

1	tablespoon water
1	teaspoon olive oil
1	cup ¾-inch cubes French bread
	salt and pepper to taste

SALAD

8	cups torn romaine
	pepper to taste
	freshly grated Parmesan cheese to taste

For the dressing, process the wine vinegar, cheese, olive oil, onion, garlic, capers, Dijon mustard, salt and pepper in a blender container until smooth.

For the croutons, mix the water and olive oil in a 9x13-inch baking pan. Add the bread cubes and toss gently to coat. Spread the bread cubes in a single layer in the pan. Season with salt and pepper. Bake at 400 degrees for 10 to 15 minutes or until crisp and golden brown. Cool in the pan.

For the salad, place the lettuce in a large salad bowl. Sprinkle generously with pepper. Add the dressing, tossing to coat. Sprinkle with cheese and top with the croutons.

YIELD: 4 SERVINGS

Nutrients Per Serving: Cal 117; Prot 4 g; Carbo 8 g; T Fat 8 g;
(Saturated Fat 2 g); Chol 2 mg; Fiber 2 g; Sod 188 mg

ENTREES

ENTREES

Mongolian Beef

⅓	cup reduced-sodium soy sauce
¼	cup balsamic vinegar
¼	cup red wine vinegar
2	tablespoons minced garlic
1	tablespoon hoisin sauce
2	teaspoons minced gingerroot
¼	teaspoon crushed red pepper
1	teaspoon canola oil
1	pound beef tenderloin, trimmed, sliced paper-thin
	tops of 12 green onions, cut into 2-inch pieces
4	cups hot cooked rice

Combine the soy sauce, balsamic vinegar, wine vinegar, garlic, hoisin sauce, gingerroot and red pepper in a bowl and mix well. Heat the canola oil in a nonstick skillet over medium heat. Add the beef gradually.

Cook just until brown, stirring frequently. Stir in the soy sauce mixture. Cook for 10 minutes or until thickened, stirring frequently. Stir in the green onion tops. Cook for 5 minutes longer or until the tops are limp, stirring occasionally. Spoon over the hot rice on a serving platter.

YIELD: 4 SERVINGS

Nutrients Per Serving: Cal 454; Prot 31 g; Carbo 55 g; T Fat 10 g;
(Saturated Fat 3 g); Chol 71 mg; Fiber 1 g; Sod 799 mg

Citrus-Grilled Flank Steak

1	(1-pound) flank steak
1	cup orange juice
⅓	cup lemon juice
3	tablespoons Worcestershire sauce
1	tablespoon canola oil
3	garlic cloves, minced
1	teaspoon cumin
¾	teaspoon onion powder
½	teaspoon salt
½	teaspoon pepper

Place the steak in a sealable plastic bag. Combine the orange juice, lemon juice, Worcestershire sauce, canola oil, garlic, cumin, onion powder, salt and pepper in a bowl and mix well. Pour over the steak and seal the bag. Marinate in the refrigerator for 2 to 10 hours, turning occasionally; drain.

Grill the steak over medium-high coals for 5 to 6 minutes per side or until the desired degree of doneness (145 degrees for medium rare, 160 degrees for medium, 170 degrees for well-done). Remove to a platter. Slice the steak diagonally against the grain. Serve immediately.

YIELD: 4 SERVINGS

Nutrients Per Serving: Cal 256; Prot 24 g; Carbo 11 g; T Fat 12 g; (Saturated Fat 4 g); Chol 59 mg; Fiber <1 g; Sod 489 mg
Nutritional information includes the entire amount of marinade.

Marinades can improve the tenderness and flavor of lean cuts of meats. Try marinades that contain citrus juices, wine, fat-free salad dressings, or buttermilk.

Grilled Steak Bruschetta

This great steak sandwich is an adaptation of a winning recipe from a National Beef Cook-Off®.

1	(12-ounce) beef top sirloin steak, trimmed
1	envelope Italian salad dressing mix
4	(6-inch) steak rolls, split
¾	cup shredded part-skim mozzarella cheese
2	cups julienned fresh spinach
1	large tomato, chopped
⅓	cup julienned fresh basil

Pat both sides of the steak with the dressing mix. Grill the steak over hot coals for 5 to 6 minutes per side or until the desired degree of doneness (145 degrees for medium rare, 160 degrees for medium, 170 degrees for well-done). Grill the rolls cut side down for 1 to 2 minutes or until golden brown. Sprinkle the toasted side with the cheese. Grill until the cheese melts.

Toss the spinach, tomato and basil in a bowl. Place equal amounts of the spinach mixture on the bottom half of each roll. Slice the steak against the grain into thin strips. Arrange over the top of the spinach mixture. Top with the remaining roll halves.

YIELD: 4 SERVINGS

Nutrients Per Serving: Cal 452; Prot 34 g; Carbo 48 g; T Fat 14 g; (Saturated Fat 7 g); Chol 68 mg; Fiber 3 g; Sod 1211 mg

Beef Burgundy

This slow-cooker recipe is great when company is expected and you don't have much time to cook.

2	pounds lean sirloin or round steak, cut into 1-inch cubes
¼	cup flour
1	teaspoon canola oil
1	cup beef broth
1	cup burgundy or other red wine
2	teaspoons thyme
1	teaspoon marjoram
½	teaspoon salt
¼	teaspoon pepper
8	ounces fresh mushrooms, sliced
2	tablespoons cornstarch
2	tablespoons cold water

Coat the steak with the flour. Heat the canola oil in a large nonstick skillet over medium heat. Add the steak. Cook until brown on both sides. Combine the beef, broth, wine, thyme, marjoram, salt and pepper in a slow cooker and mix well.

Cook, covered, on Low for 6 to 8 hours or until of the desired consistency, adding the mushrooms and a mixture of the cornstarch and cold water during the last 30 minutes of the cooking process and mixing well. Spoon over hot fettuccini or rice on a serving platter.

YIELD: 6 SERVINGS

Nutrients Per Serving: Cal 307; Prot 37 g; Carbo 8 g; T Fat 10 g; (Saturated Fat 4 g); Chol 102 mg; Fiber 1 g; Sod 404 mg

Use lean well-trimmed cuts of meat, such as round or loin cuts. Remove excess fat and poultry skin and enhance the flavor with herbs, spices, and marinades.

Savory Stuffed Peppers Italian-Style

4	large green bell peppers
5	cups boiling water
8	ounces 93% to 95% lean ground beef
1	small onion, chopped
2	cups cooked brown rice
1	(8-ounce) can tomato sauce
1	teaspoon Worcestershire sauce
$\frac{1}{2}$	teaspoon salt
$\frac{1}{8}$	teaspoon garlic powder
2	(8-ounce) cans tomato sauce
2	teaspoons Italian seasoning
2	tablespoons grated Parmesan cheese

Cut the green peppers lengthwise into halves. Discard the seeds and membranes. Pour the boiling water over the green peppers in a heatproof bowl. Let stand for 5 minutes; drain. Plunge the green peppers into cold water in a bowl to stop the cooking process; drain.

Cook the ground beef with the onion in a skillet, stirring until the ground beef is brown throughout, and juices show no pink color; drain. Blot the ground beef mixture with a paper towel. Stir in the brown rice, 1 can tomato sauce, Worcestershire sauce, salt and garlic powder.

Mound about ½ cup of the ground beef mixture in each green pepper half. Arrange the peppers stuffing side up in an ungreased 9x13-inch baking dish. Pour a mixture of 2 cans tomato sauce and Italian seasoning over the peppers. Bake, covered, at 350 degrees for 40 to 45 minutes; remove cover. Sprinkle with the cheese. Bake for 10 to 15 minutes longer or until brown.

YIELD: 8 SERVINGS

Nutrients Per Serving: **Cal 153; Prot 10 g; Carbo 23 g; T Fat 3 g; (Saturated Fat 1 g); Chol 13 mg; Fiber 4 g; Sod 715 mg**

Spinach Enchilada Casserole

1	(10-ounce) package frozen chopped spinach, thawed, rinsed, drained
1½	pounds lean ground beef
½	cup chopped onion
½	cup chopped green bell pepper
1	garlic clove, minced
1	(8-ounce) can tomato sauce
2	tomatoes, chopped
2	(4-ounce) cans chopped green chiles
1	tablespoon lime juice
1	tablespoon sugar
12	(6-inch) corn tortillas
1	cup fat-free sour cream
3	cups shredded reduced-fat Monterey Jack cheese
	sliced black olives (optional)

Squeeze the excess moisture from the spinach. Cook the ground beef with the onion, green pepper and garlic in a skillet, stirring until the ground beef is brown throughout, and juices show no pink color; drain. Stir in the spinach, tomato sauce, tomatoes, chiles, lime juice and sugar. Simmer for 10 minutes, stirring occasionally.

Spray a 9x13-inch baking pan with nonstick cooking spray. Layer the tortillas, ground beef mixture, sour cream and cheese ½ at a time in the prepared baking pan. Bake at 350 degrees for 30 to 40 minutes or until bubbly. Sprinkle with black olives.

YIELD: 12 SERVINGS

Nutrients Per Serving: Cal 311; Prot 24 g; Carbo 22 g; T Fat 14 g; (Saturated Fat 6 g); Chol 56 mg; Fiber 3 g; Sod 623 mg

Teriyaki Miniature Meat Loaves

1¾ pounds lean ground beef
½ cup dry bread crumbs
½ cup honey-teriyaki barbecue sauce
1 egg, beaten
¼ teaspoon pepper
½ cup honey-teriyaki barbecue sauce
6 fresh mushrooms, sliced

Spray twelve 2½-inch muffin cups with nonstick cooking spray. Combine the ground beef, bread crumbs, ½ cup barbecue sauce, egg and pepper in a bowl and mix just until combined. Spoon the ground beef mixture into the prepared muffin cups and press lightly.

Combine ½ cup barbecue sauce and mushrooms in a bowl and mix well. Spoon over the tops of the meat loaves. Bake at 400 degrees for 20 to 25 minutes or until the meat mixture registers 160 degrees in the center.

YIELD: 12 MEAT LOAVES

Nutrients Per Serving: Cal 210; Prot 16 g; Carbo 11 g; T Fat 10 g; (Saturated Fat 4 g); Chol 65 mg; Fiber <1 g, Sod 497 mg

Grilled Lamb with Garlic Rub

3 garlic cloves, minced
3 tablespoons minced fresh rosemary
1½ teaspoons salt
1 teaspoon pepper
zest of 1 lemon
4 (4- to 5-ounce) lamb loin chops

Combine the garlic, rosemary, salt, pepper and lemon zest in a bowl, stirring until of the consistency of a paste. Rub both sides of the lamb chops with the paste. Grill the lamb chops over medium-high coals for 5 to 6 minutes per side or until the desired degree of doneness is reached when measured in the center of each chop (145 degrees for medium rare, 160 degrees for medium, 170 degrees for well-done). May broil for 4 to 6 minutes per side or until of the desired degree of doneness.

YIELD: 4 SERVINGS

Nutrients Per Serving: Cal 250; Prot 34 g; Carbo 2 g; T Fat 11 g; (Saturated Fat 4 g); Chol 106 mg; Fiber <1 g; Sod 967 mg

Jalapeño Honey Pork Tenderloin

⅓	cup honey
3	tablespoons reduced-sodium soy sauce
1	tablespoon sesame oil
2	jalapeño chiles, seeded, finely chopped
1	tablespoon grated gingerroot
¼	teaspoon red pepper flakes
2	(12-ounce) pork tenderloins

Combine the honey, soy sauce, sesame oil, chiles, gingerroot and red pepper flakes in a 1-gallon sealable plastic bag. Add the pork and seal tightly. Shake to coat. Marinate in the refrigerator for 8 hours, turning occasionally; drain.

Grill the pork over medium-hot coals until a meat thermometer inserted in the thickest portion of the pork registers 160 degrees. Remove the pork to a serving platter. Cut diagonally into ¼-inch slices. Let stand, covered, for 10 minutes before serving.

Tip: If you do not have access to a grill, or prefer to cook indoors, place the pork on a rack in a roasting pan. Bake at 425 degrees for 40 minutes or until a meat thermometer registers 160 degrees.

YIELD: 6 SERVINGS

Nutrients Per Serving: Cal 228; Prot 25 g; Carbo 17 g; T Fat 6 g; (Saturated Fat 2 g); Chol 67 mg; Fiber <1 g; Sod 302 mg
Nutritional information includes the entire amount of marinade.

Wear latex gloves to keep the oil off your hands when chopping or working with jalapeño chiles or any type of hot peppers. Your skin, especially around the eyes, is very sensitive to the oil from the hot peppers.

Grilled Pork Chops with Cherry Almond Sauce

⅔   cup cherry preserves
2   tablespoons red wine vinegar
⅛   teaspoon cinnamon
⅛   teaspoon ground cloves
⅛   teaspoon nutmeg
2   tablespoons sliced blanched almonds
4   (4-ounce) pork loin chops, ½ inch thick

Combine the preserves, wine vinegar, cinnamon, cloves and nutmeg in a saucepan and mix well. Bring to a boil. Boil for 1 minute, stirring occasionally. Remove from heat. Stir in the almonds. Pour ⅓ of mixture into a glass measure to use for basting. Reserve the remainder to serve as a sauce with the chops.

Grill the pork chops 4 to 6 inches from the heat source over medium-hot coals for 4 to 5 minutes on one side. Turn and grill on the other side, basting with the cherry almond sauce. Continue grilling until the desired degree of doneness is reached when measured in the center of each chop (145 degrees for medium rare; 160 degrees for medium, 170 degrees for well-done). Serve with the reserved cherry almond sauce.

YIELD: 4 SERVINGS

Nutrients Per Serving: Cal 296; Prot 23 g; Carbo 35 g; T Fat 7 g; (Saturated Fat 2 g); Chol 57 mg; Fiber 1 g; Sod 59 mg

Oriental Fruited Pork

1	(16-ounce) can apricot halves in light syrup
1½	teaspoons cornstarch
4	pork loin chops, ½ inch thick
2	tablespoons reduced-sodium soy sauce
1	tablespoon cornstarch
1	teaspoon sesame oil
¼	teaspoon black pepper
	crushed red pepper to taste
1	teaspoon peanut oil
1	(10-ounce) package frozen snow peas, partially thawed
¼	cup water
1	teaspoon peanut oil
3	cups cooked rice

Drain the apricots, reserving ⅓ cup of the syrup. Stir 1½ teaspoons cornstarch into the reserved syrup in a bowl. Trim the bone and fat from the pork chops and discard. Pound the pork ¼ inch thick between sheets of waxed paper. Cut the pork into ½x1-inch cubes.

Combine the soy sauce, 1 tablespoon cornstarch, sesame oil, black pepper and red pepper in a bowl and mix well. Add the pork, tossing to coat. Let stand at room temperature for 15 minutes, stirring occasionally.

Heat 1 teaspoon peanut oil in a wok over high heat. Add the snow peas. Stir-fry for 30 seconds. Add the water. Steam, covered, for 1 minute. Remove the snow peas to a platter.

Heat 1 teaspoon peanut oil in the wok over high heat. Add the pork. Stir-fry for 3 to 4 minutes. Add the apricots and snow peas and mix well. Stir-fry for 30 seconds. Stir in the reserved syrup mixture. Cook until thickened, stirring constantly. Spoon the pork mixture over the rice on a serving platter.

YIELD: 4 SERVINGS

Nutrients Per Serving: Cal 434; Prot 27 g; Carbo 61 g; T Fat 9 g; (Saturated Fat 2 g); Chol 51 mg; Fiber 5 g; Sod 303 mg

Pork Souvlaki Kabobs

3	tablespoons olive oil
3	tablespoons fresh lemon juice
1	teaspoon oregano
1/8	teaspoon pepper
1/4	teaspoon garlic powder
2	(4-ounce) lean pork loin chops, cut into 1-inch cubes
1	medium onion, cut into 1-inch squares
1	medium red bell pepper, cut into 1-inch squares

Combine the olive oil, lemon juice, oregano, pepper and garlic powder in a bowl and mix well. Reserve 1/4 cup of the marinade. Add the pork to the remaining marinade, tossing to coat. Marinate, covered, in the refrigerator for 1 hour or longer, stirring occasionally.

Thread the onion, red pepper and pork alternately on four 12-inch bamboo skewers. Grill the kabobs over medium-hot coals for 15 to 20 minutes or until the pork is cooked through and the vegetables are tender, basting with the reserved marinade frequently.

Tip: Soak the bamboo skewers in water while the pork is marinating. This will prevent the skewers from charring or catching on fire during the grilling process.

YIELD: 4 KABOBS

Nutrients Per Kabob: Cal 183; Prot 12 g; Carbo 5 g; T Fat 13 g; (Saturated Fat 2 g); Chol 29 mg; Fiber 1 g; Sod 25 mg
Nutritional information includes the entire amount of marinade.

Many labels, especially on meat, fish, and poultry, offer excellent guidelines for handling, storing, and cooking safety measures.

Mile-High Marinara and Prosciutto

1	teaspoon olive oil
½	cup chopped onion
2	garlic cloves, minced
1	(28-ounce) can crushed Italian tomatoes in purée
½	cup chopped prosciutto
½	cup chopped fresh basil
¼	teaspoon crushed red pepper flakes
1	medium tomato, chopped
¼	cup grated Parmesan cheese
1	egg, beaten
4	cups cooked spaghetti

Heat the olive oil in a medium nonstick skillet. Add the onion and garlic. Sauté until the onion is tender. Stir in the undrained cannned tomatoes, prosciutto, basil and red pepper flakes.

Cook over medium heat for 10 minutes, stirring occasionally. Add the fresh tomato and cheese and mix well. Cook for 5 minutes, stirring frequently. Whisk in the egg gradually. Cook for 1 minute longer. Spoon over the spaghetti on a serving platter.

Tip: May substitute chopped Canadian bacon for the prosciutto and 4 teaspoons dried basil for the fresh basil.

YIELD: 4 SERVINGS

Nutrients Per Serving: Cal 363; Prot 19 g; Carbo 58 g; T Fat 7 g; (Saturated Fat 2 g); Chol 68 mg; Fiber 7 g; Sod 631 mg

Home-Style Skillet Chicken

An easy replacement for fried chicken.

1	(3-pound) chicken, cut up
⅓	cup flour
½	teaspoon salt
½	teaspoon paprika
½	teaspoon poultry seasoning
¼	teaspoon onion powder
⅛	teaspoon pepper
1	tablespoon canola oil
½	cup water

Remove the skin and all visible fat from the chicken. Combine the flour, salt, paprika, poultry seasoning, onion powder and pepper in a large sealable plastic bag. Seal the bag and shake to mix. Add the chicken 1 or 2 pieces at a time. Seal the bag and shake to coat. Place the chicken on a sheet of waxed paper.

Heat the canola oil in a large nonstick skillet until hot. Add the chicken. Cook over medium heat for 10 minutes per side or until brown. Add the water. Cook, covered, over low heat for 30 minutes or until the chicken is cooked through.

Tip: The pan drippings may be used to make gravy for mashed potatoes.

YIELD: 4 SERVINGS

Nutrients Per Serving: Cal 308; Prot 37 g; Carbo 8 g; T Fat 13 g; (Saturated Fat 3 g); Chol 108 mg; Fiber <1 g; Sod 399 mg

Chicken Breasts with Herb Sauce

4	boneless skinless chicken breast halves
2	tablespoons butter or margarine
⅓	cup lemon juice
1	teaspoon celery salt
1	teaspoon dry mustard
1	teaspoon garlic powder
1	teaspoon paprika
½	teaspoon pepper
2	tablespoons grated Parmesan cheese
2	teaspoons parsley flakes

Pound the chicken ½ inch thick between sheets of waxed paper. Arrange in a single layer in a large baking dish.

Heat the butter in a small saucepan until melted. Stir in the lemon juice, celery salt, dry mustard, garlic powder, paprika and pepper. Cook over medium heat for 1 minute, stirring occasionally.

Drizzle the butter mixture over the chicken. Sprinkle with the cheese and parsley flakes. Bake at 300 degrees for 50 to 60 minutes or until the chicken is cooked through.

YIELD: 4 SERVINGS

Nutrients Per Serving: Cal 359; Prot 55 g; Carbo 2 g; T Fat 13 g; (Saturated Fat 6 g); Chol 164 mg; Fiber <1 g; Sod 616 mg

When cooking meat and poultry, the best way to judge doneness and ensure food has reached a safe temperature is by using a thermometer. Large oven-proof thermometers work well for whole turkeys and roasts. Disposable temperature sticks and instant-read dial or digital thermometers work better for steaks, hamburgers and chicken pieces. →

Chicken Oregano

¼ cup lemon juice
1 tablespoon olive oil
1 teaspoon oregano
½ teaspoon pepper
½ teaspoon salt
1 garlic clove, minced
4 boneless skinless chicken breast halves

Whisk the lemon juice, olive oil, oregano, pepper, salt and garlic in a bowl. Pour over the chicken in a 1-gallon sealable plastic bag and seal tightly. Shake to coat.

Marinate the chicken in the refrigerator for 2 to 10 hours, turning occasionally. Grill over medium-high heat for 5 minutes; turn. Grill for 5 minutes longer or until the chicken is cooked through.

YIELD: 4 SERVINGS

Nutrients Per Serving: Cal 319; Prot 53 g; Carbo 2 g; T Fat 10 g; (Saturated Fat 2 g); Chol 146 mg; Fiber <1 g; Sod 418 mg

The following end-point temperatures are recommended:

145°F: Medium-rare beef, veal or lamb; Fish fillets

160°F: All ground meat and meat mixtures; Medium beef, veal, lamb or pork; Fresh ham; Egg dishes

165°F: Ground poultry; Stuffing mixtures

170°F: Poultry breasts and roasts; Well done beef, veal, lamb, and pork

180°F: Whole chicken, turkey, duck and goose; Poultry thighs and wings

Chicken Tortilla Casserole

1   pound boneless skinless chicken breasts
1   (10-ounce) can reduced-fat cream of chicken soup
1   (10-ounce) can reduced-fat cream of mushroom soup
4   (12-inch) flour tortillas
1   medium onion, cut into 1-inch strips
2   large green bell peppers, cut into 1-inch strips
1   (10-ounce) can diced tomatoes with green chiles
1½ cups shredded reduced-fat Cheddar cheese

Combine the chicken with enough water to cover in a saucepan. Cook until tender. Drain, reserving ½ cup of the stock. Shred the chicken. Combine the soups with the reserved stock in a bowl and mix well.

Layer the tortillas, chicken, onion, green peppers, soup mixture, undrained tomatoes and cheese ½ at a time in a 9x13-inch baking pan sprayed with nonstick cooking spray. Bake at 350 degrees for 30 to 40 minutes or until bubbly.

Tip: You can enjoy foods that are a little higher in sodium content—this recipe, for example—and still follow a reduced-sodium diet. Just be sure to choose foods that are naturally low in sodium, such as a salad or fresh steamed vegetables, to round out the meal and even out the overall sodium content.

YIELD: 8 SERVINGS

Nutrients Per Serving: Cal 325; Prot 23 g; Carbo 35 g; T Fat 10 g; (Saturated Fat 4 g); Chol 48 mg; Fiber 3 g; Sod 788 mg

Grilling meats and vegetables can add a wonderful robust flavor, although heavy consumption of charred foods has been linked to cancer. While the risk is low for those who use their grills occasionally, here are a few tips for using your grill safely:
*
Avoid burning or charring your grilled foods. →

Herb Mustard Grilled Chicken

⅓   cup lemon juice

¼   cup Dijon mustard

1   tablespoon finely chopped fresh parsley

2   teaspoons whole basil

2   teaspoons grated lemon zest

1   teaspoon vegetable oil

    salt and pepper to taste

4   chicken breast halves, skinned

Whisk the lemon juice, Dijon mustard, parsley, basil, lemon zest, oil, salt and pepper in a bowl. Pour over the chicken in a shallow dish, turning to coat.

Marinate, covered, in the refrigerator for 4 to 10 hours, turning occasionally. Grill the chicken over hot coals for 5 to 6 minutes per side or until cooked through.

YIELD: 4 SERVINGS

Nutrients Per Serving: **Cal 319; Prot 54 g; Carbo 4 g; T Fat 9 g; (Saturated Fat 2 g); Chol 146 mg; Fiber <1 g; Sod 507 mg**

*
Choose lean cuts of meat; remove visible fat from poultry and avoid fatty marinades.
*
Grill a variety of foods—vegetables, pizza crusts, and even fruit are examples of reduced-fat foods that are ideal cooked on the grill.

Lemon Chicken with Fettuccini

8	ounces fettuccini
2	boneless skinless chicken breast halves
½	teaspoon lemon pepper
2	garlic cloves, minced
1	tablespoon canola oil
¼	cup lemon juice
	black pepper to taste
2	tablespoons chopped fresh parsley
2	tablespoons grated Parmesan cheese

Cook the pasta using package directions; drain. Cover to keep warm. Sprinkle both sides of the chicken with the lemon pepper. Grill the chicken over hot coals for 4 to 5 minutes per side or until cooked through. Cut the chicken into strips. Cover to keep warm.

Sauté the garlic in the canola oil in a saucepan for 1 minute. Stir in the lemon juice and black pepper. Cook until heated through, stirring constantly. Add to the pasta, tossing to coat.

Spoon the pasta onto a serving platter. Top with the chicken. Sprinkle with the parsley and cheese. Serve immediately.

YIELD: 4 SERVINGS

Nutrients Per Serving: Cal 347; Prot 34 g; Carbo 34 g; T Fat 9 g; (Saturated Fat 2 g); Chol 76 mg; Fiber 2 g; Sod 282 mg

Plum-Glazed Chicken Kabobs

½	cup plum jam
¼	cup chopped green onions
2	tablespoons reduced-sodium soy sauce
2	tablespoons chili sauce
1	teaspoon minced garlic
1	teaspoon minced gingerroot
2	pounds boneless skinless chicken breasts, cut into 1-inch pieces
8	ounces zucchini, cut into 1-inch slices
1	red onion, cut into large chunks
12	mushroom caps

 Combine the jam, green onions, soy sauce, chili sauce, garlic and gingerroot in a bowl and mix well. Add the chicken, tossing to coat. Marinate, covered, in the refrigerator for 15 minutes to several hours, stirring occasionally. Drain, discarding the marinade.

Thread the chicken, zucchini, red onion and mushrooms alternately on skewers until all of the ingredients are used. Grill over hot coals for 5 minutes per side or until the chicken is cooked through and the vegetables are tender. Serve over rice pilaf.

YIELD: 6 SERVINGS

Nutrients Per Serving: **Cal 271; Prot 32 g; Carbo 23 g; T Fat 4 g; (Saturated Fat 1 g); Chol 84 mg; Fiber 1 g; Sod 333 mg Nutritional information includes the entire amount of marinade.**

Use separate cutting boards for uncooked meats and other foods. Clean the cutting boards thoroughly with hot water and soap and then rinse with bleach or a sanitizing solution.

Baked Sour Cream Chicken

1½   cups fat-free sour cream
½   teaspoon paprika
½   teaspoon salt
½   teaspoon tarragon
½   teaspoon thyme
½   teaspoon garlic powder
6   chicken breast halves, skinned
1½   cups cornflake crumbs

Combine the sour cream, paprika, salt, tarragon, thyme and garlic powder in a bowl and mix well. Coat the chicken with the sour cream mixture and roll in the cornflake crumbs.

Arrange the chicken in a single layer in a 9x13-inch baking pan sprayed with nonstick cooking spray. Bake at 350 degrees for 40 to 50 minutes or until the chicken is cooked through.

YIELD: 6 SERVINGS

Nutrients Per Serving: Cal 426; Prot 59 g; Carbo 29 g; T Fat 6 g; (Saturated Fat 2 g); Chol 146 mg; Fiber 0 g; Sod 605 mg

In most dishes that call for sour cream, substituting fat-free yogurt can save 350 calories per cup. To keep yogurt from separating in cooked dishes or those that will be stirred, combine one tablespoon cornstarch with one tablespoon of the yogurt and stir into the remaining yogurt and then into the recipe.

Thai Chicken and Noodles

1	pound boneless skinless chicken breasts
¾	cup reduced-fat Italian salad dressing
8	ounces angel hair pasta
2	tablespoons peanut butter
1	tablespoon reduced-sodium soy sauce
1	tablespoon honey
1½	teaspoons freshly grated gingerroot
½	teaspoon crushed red pepper
1	teaspoon vegetable oil
1	teaspoon sesame oil
¾	cup shredded carrot
¾	cup snow peas, trimmed
1	cup chopped green onions
2	tablespoons chopped fresh cilantro

Cut the chicken diagonally into thin strips. Combine the chicken and ¼ cup of the salad dressing in a bowl and mix well. Marinate, covered, in the refrigerator for 1 hour, stirring occasionally.

Cook the pasta using package directions; drain. Whisk the remaining ½ cup salad dressing, peanut butter, soy sauce, honey, gingerroot and red pepper in a bowl until mixed.

Drain the chicken, discarding the marinade. Heat the vegetable oil in a large nonstick skillet or wok over high heat. Add the chicken. Stir-fry for 3 minutes. Add the sesame oil, carrot, snow peas and green onions and mix well. Stir-fry for 3 minutes longer or until the chicken is cooked through and the vegetables are tender. Reduce the heat to low.

Add the pasta, salad dressing mixture and cilantro to the chicken mixture and toss to mix. Cook just until heated through, stirring constantly. Spoon onto a serving platter. Garnish with additional chopped cilantro.

YIELD: 6 SERVINGS

Nutrients Per Serving: Cal 274; Prot 22 g; Carbo 30 g; T Fat 7 g; (Saturated Fat 1 g); Chol 42 mg; Fiber 2 g; Sod 780 mg
Nutritional information includes the entire amount of salad dressing.

Vegetable Chicken Lasagna

A great lasagna that also works well with turkey leftovers.

8	ounces lasagna noodles
1	(10-ounce) package frozen chopped spinach, thawed, drained
15	ounces fat-free ricotta cheese
1	egg, beaten
4	boneless skinless chicken breast halves, cubed
3	cups sliced fresh mushrooms
1	medium onion, chopped
2	garlic cloves, minced
1	tablespoon Italian seasoning
1	tablespoon olive oil
1	(28-ounce) can Italian-style chopped tomatoes
1	(15-ounce) can tomato sauce
2	cups shredded carrots
½	teaspoon pepper
6	ounces part-skim mozzarella cheese, shredded
¼	cup grated Parmesan cheese

Cook the noodles using package directions; drain. Squeeze the excess moisture from the spinach. Combine the spinach, ricotta cheese and egg in a bowl and mix well. Chill, covered, in the refrigerator until needed.

Sauté the chicken, mushrooms, onion, garlic and Italian seasoning in the olive oil in a skillet until the chicken turns white. Stir in the undrained tomatoes, tomato sauce, carrots and pepper. Simmer for 5 minutes or until the chicken is cooked through, stirring occasionally.

Layer the noodles, spinach mixture, chicken mixture, mozzarella cheese and Parmesan cheese ½ at a time in a 9x13-inch baking dish sprayed with nonstick cooking spray. Bake, covered, at 350 degrees for 25 to 30 minutes or until bubbly; remove cover. Bake for 10 minutes longer or until the cheese melts.

YIELD: 8 SERVINGS

Nutrients Per Serving: Cal 368; Prot 43 g; Carbo 24 g; T Fat 10 g; (Saturated Fat 4 g); Chol 114 mg; Fiber 4 g; Sod 814 mg

Cranberry Chicken and Wild Rice

1	(6-ounce) package long grain and wild rice with seasoning packet
½	cup long grain rice
2	cups water
1	(16-ounce) can whole cranberry sauce
2	tablespoons reduced-sodium soy sauce
1	tablespoon lemon juice
½	cup water
¼	cup flour
6	boneless skinless chicken breast halves
¼	cup sliced almonds

Combine 6 ounces long grain and wild rice and ½ cup long grain rice in a 3-quart baking dish and mix well. Spread evenly over the bottom of the dish. Sprinkle with the seasoning packet.

Combine 2 cups water, cranberry sauce, soy sauce and lemon juice in a saucepan and mix well. Cook over medium heat until the cranberry sauce melts, stirring occasionally. Whisk ½ cup water and flour in a bowl until smooth. Stir into the cranberry sauce mixture.

Spoon half the cranberry sauce mixture over the rice. Arrange the chicken over the prepared layers. Top with the remaining cranberry sauce mixture. Bake, covered, at 350 degrees for 1 hour or until the chicken is cooked through and the rice is tender; remove cover. Sprinkle with the almonds. Bake for 10 minutes longer.

YIELD: 6 SERVINGS

Nutrients Per Serving: Cal 598; Prot 59 g; Carbo 68 g; T Fat 9 g; (Saturated Fat 2 g); Chol 146 mg; Fiber 2 g; Sod 734 mg

Ginger Chicken Wraps

GINGER SLAW

3	tablespoons rice vinegar
1	tablespoon vegetable oil
1	tablespoon sugar
2	teaspoons teriyaki sauce
2	teaspoons minced jalapeño chile
1	teaspoon freshly grated gingerroot
1	(16-ounce) package coleslaw mix

CHICKEN WRAPS

1	pound chicken tenderloins
¼	cup teriyaki sauce
1	tablespoon minced garlic
1	teaspoon vegetable oil
2	cups cooked rice
4	(10-inch) flour tortillas, heated
1	cup chopped fresh cilantro

For the slaw, whisk the rice vinegar, oil, sugar, teriyaki sauce, chile and gingerroot in a bowl. Add the coleslaw mix and toss to coat.

For the wraps, combine the chicken, teriyaki sauce and garlic in a bowl and mix well. Marinate in the refrigerator for 10 minutes; drain. Pat the chicken with paper towels. Heat the oil in a nonstick skillet. Add the chicken. Cook for 5 to 7 minutes or until cooked through and brown on both sides, stirring frequently. Spoon ¼ of the rice down the center of each tortilla. Spoon ¼ of the slaw on 1 side of the rice. Arrange the chicken and cilantro next to the slaw. Fold in the sides of the tortillas and roll to enclose the filling. Cut each wrap into halves before serving.

YIELD: 4 SERVINGS

Nutrients Per Serving: Cal 570; Prot 33 g; Carbo 78 g; T Fat 13 g;
(Saturated Fat 3 g); Chol 63 mg; Fiber 3 g; Sod 1251 mg
Nutritional information includes the entire amount of marinade.

Peppery Turkey Breast with Pineapple Cranberry Relish

PINEAPPLE CRANBERRY RELISH

12	ounces fresh or frozen cranberries
1	(8-ounce) can juice-pack crushed pineapple
1	cup sugar
¼	cup orange juice
2	teaspoons vanilla extract
1	teaspoon grated orange zest

TURKEY

1	(3-pound) boneless turkey breast
1	teaspoon seasoned salt
1	teaspoon white pepper

For the relish, combine the cranberries, undrained pineapple, ¾ cup of the sugar and orange juice in a food processor container. Process until coarsely chopped. Pour into a nonreactive saucepan. Bring to a boil over medium heat, stirring occasionally; reduce heat.

Simmer for 10 to 12 minutes or until thickened, stirring occasionally. Stir in the remaining ¼ cup sugar. Remove from heat. Stir in the vanilla and orange zest. Transfer to a glass or plastic bowl. Cool to room temperature. Chill, covered, until serving time.

For the turkey, pat the surface of the turkey with the seasoned salt and white pepper. Arrange the turkey in a baking dish and cover with foil.

Insert a meat thermometer through the foil into the thickest portion of the turkey. Bake at 325 degrees for 25 to 30 minutes per pound or until thermometer registers 170 degrees when measured in center of breast. Slice and serve with the chilled relish.

YIELD: 6 SERVINGS

Nutrients Per Serving: Cal 452; Prot 60 g; Carbo 48 g; T Fat 2 g; (Saturated Fat <1 g); Chol 164 mg; Fiber 3 g; Sod 257 mg

Seventy-five percent of teenage girls, as well as many older folks, are deficient in iron and zinc. Lean red meats and skinless poultry offer both minerals—plus they're quick, flavorful, and easy to cook when you are in a hurry. Other sources include fortified cereals, dried beans, and enriched grain products.

Orange Roughy Mediterranean-Style

1	tablespoon olive oil
¾	cup finely chopped onion
3	garlic cloves, minced
2	(14-ounce) cans diced tomatoes in juice
½	cup dry white wine
1	(10-ounce) package fresh spinach, rinsed, drained
2	tablespoons lemon juice
1	tablespoon parsley flakes
2	teaspoons basil
2	teaspoons dillweed
6	(4-ounce) orange roughy fillets, rinsed, drained
½	teaspoon white pepper
¼	cup capers

Heat the olive oil in a large nonstick skillet. Add the onion and garlic. Sauté for 5 minutes or just until the onion begins to soften. Stir in the undrained tomatoes and white wine. Cook over medium heat for 10 minutes, stirring occasionally. Stir in the spinach.

Cook, covered, for 3 to 5 minutes or until the spinach is slightly wilted. Remove from heat. Stir in the lemon juice, parsley flakes, basil and dillweed.

Spoon half the spinach mixture into a 9x13-inch baking dish sprayed with nonstick cooking spray. Arrange the fillets over the prepared layer. Sprinkle with the white pepper. Top with the remaining spinach mixture. Sprinkle with the capers. Bake, covered, at 400 degrees for 15 minutes or until the fish flakes easily. Serve over hot cooked rice or pasta.

YIELD: 6 SERVINGS

Nutrients Per Serving: Cal 164; Prot 20 g; Carbo 10 g; T Fat 3 g; (Saturated Fat <1 g); Chol 24 mg; Fiber 3 g; Sod 509 mg

Salmon Loaf

An easy way to incorporate omega-3 fatty acids into your diet. The tiny soft bones found in canned salmon are completely edible and are a source of calcium.

1	(16-ounce) can red salmon, drained
½	cup reduced-fat sour cream
1	small onion, chopped
2	eggs, lightly beaten
	juice of ½ medium lemon
6	saltine crackers, crushed
¼	teaspoon pepper
2	carrots, peeled, grated
¼	teaspoon paprika
2	tablespoons prepared chili sauce

Combine the salmon, sour cream, onion, eggs, lemon juice, crackers and pepper in a bowl and mix well. Spread in a lightly greased 9-inch round baking pan. Sprinkle with the carrots and paprika.

Bake at 350 degrees for 40 to 45 minutes or until light brown. Cut into 6 wedges. Top each wedge with 1 teaspoon of the chili sauce.

YIELD: 6 SERVINGS

Nutrients Per Serving: Cal 219; Prot 20 g; Carbo 9 g; T Fat 12 g;
(Saturated Fat 3 g); Chol 125 mg; Fiber 1 g; Sod 483 mg

Salmon en Papillote

Opening these packets reveals a delicious dinner.

2	(4- to 6-ounce) salmon fillets
2	large garlic cloves, crushed
6	thin slices tomato
2	tablespoons crumbled reduced-fat feta cheese
¼	cup yellow bell pepper strips
¼	cup thinly sliced onion
1	tablespoon sliced black olives
2	teaspoons white vinegar
1	teaspoon olive oil
½	teaspoon oregano

Cut two 15-inch squares of parchment paper or foil. Fold each square in half and trim into a large heart shape. Arrange the heart shapes on 2 baking sheets and open out flat.

Place 1 salmon fillet in the center of each heart shape. Top each fillet with half the garlic, 3 tomato slices, half the feta cheese, half the yellow pepper, half the onion and half the black olives. Drizzle each with half the vinegar and half the olive oil. Sprinkle with the oregano.

Fold the edge of the parchment or foil together to seal. Bake at 450 degrees for 20 to 25 minutes or until the salmon flakes easily; packets will be slightly puffed.

Arrange 1 packet on each dinner plate. Tear or cut a slit in the top of each packet and roll the edges back. Serve immediately.

YIELD: 2 SERVINGS

Nutrients Per Serving: Cal 336; Prot 34 g; Carbo 11 g; T Fat 17 g; (Saturated Fat 3 g); Chol 104 mg; Fiber 1 g; Sod 217 mg

Glazed Salmon

1½   pounds salmon fillets
3   tablespoons reduced-sodium soy sauce
¼   cup packed brown sugar

 Arrange the salmon skin side down in a shallow dish. Drizzle with the soy sauce and sprinkle with the brown sugar; the brown sugar will absorb the soy sauce, forming a glaze. Marinate in the refrigerator for 20 minutes or longer. Drain, reserving the marinade.

Arrange the salmon skin side down on a grill rack sprayed with nonstick cooking spray. Grill over medium-high heat for 8 to 10 minutes or until the salmon flakes easily, basting with the reserved marinade; do not turn. Remove the salmon flesh from the skin, leaving the skin on the grill rack for later cleanup.

YIELD: 4 SERVINGS

Nutrients Per Serving: Cal 316; Prot 33 g; Carbo 15 g; T Fat 13 g; (Saturated Fat 2 g); Chol 102 mg; Fiber 0 g; Sod 462 mg

To keep fish from sticking to the grill rack, rub the cut side of a potato across the heated rack. The starch from the potato creates a natural nonstick coating.

Stuffed Fish Rolls

1	pound fresh mushrooms, finely chopped
½	cup minced red bell pepper
6	green onions, minced
3	garlic cloves, minced
1	tablespoon minced fresh parsley
2	teaspoons olive oil
6	(4-ounce) sole, orange roughy or any mild fish fillets
¼	teaspoon salt
½	cup dry white wine
3	tablespoons lemon juice
⅜	teaspoon lemon pepper
½	teaspoon paprika
	chopped fresh parsley to taste

Sauté the mushrooms, red pepper, green onions, garlic and 1 tablespoon parsley in the olive oil in a skillet for 5 minutes or until the vegetables are tender. Remove from heat. Season the fillets with the salt.

Spoon the mushroom mixture evenly over each fillet. Roll beginning at the small end to enclose the filling and secure with a wooden pick. Arrange the rolls in a single layer in a baking dish sprayed with nonstick cooking spray.

Combine the white wine, lemon juice and lemon pepper in a bowl and mix well. Drizzle over the fish rolls. Sprinkle with the paprika. Bake, covered, at 350 degrees for 30 to 35 minutes or until the fish flakes easily. Sprinkle with chopped fresh parsley to taste.

YIELD: 6 SERVINGS

Nutrients Per Serving: **Cal 148; Prot 22 g; Carbo 6 g; T Fat 3 g; (Saturated Fat 1 g); Chol 53 mg; Fiber 2 g; Sod 212 mg**

Good-quality flavoring ingredients are the backbone of any recipe. Following is a list of suggested ingredients to have on hand: herbs, dried and fresh; spices; vinegars—balsamic, wine, rice, apple, herb-flavored, and white; mustard—whole grain, Dijon, mustard seeds, and powder; whole peppercorns; →

Pesto Swordfish

Cooking in foil allows you to prepare the packets in advance and store them in the refrigerator until ready to grill. But the best part is the quick cleanup.

4	(6-ounce) swordfish steaks
⅓	cup white wine
2	green onions, sliced
2	garlic cloves, minced
¼	cup pesto
	salt and pepper to taste
2	medium tomatoes, chopped
1	teaspoon balsamic vinegar

 Combine the steaks, white wine, green onions and garlic in a sealable plastic bag and seal tightly. Marinate in the refrigerator for 15 minutes to 1 hour, turning occasionally.

Tear off 4 pieces of foil large enough to wrap the steaks. Place 1 steak in the middle of each piece of foil. Spread each steak with 1 tablespoon of the pesto. Sprinkle with salt and pepper. Seal the foil tightly to enclose the steaks.

Grill the packets over hot coals for 12 minutes or until the steaks flake easily. Toss the tomatoes and balsamic vinegar in a bowl. Season with salt and pepper. Remove the steaks from the foil packets and place on individual dinner plates. Top each steak with some of the tomato mixture. Serve immediately.

YIELD: 4 SERVINGS

Nutrients Per Serving: Cal 250; Prot 26 g; Carbo 5 g; T Fat 12 g; (Saturated Fat 3 g); Chol 50 mg; Fiber 1 g; Sod 218 mg

tomatoes—fresh (in season), roasted or pan-smoked for flavor, canned, and sun-dried; chocolate— Dutch-processed cocoa powder and a variety of baking chocolates; extracts—vanilla, almond, and lemon; vanilla beans and vanilla powder; and a selection of wine, liqueurs, and cordials.

Pumpkin Seed Trout

Pumpkin seeds are a satisfying accompaniment to this Rocky Mountain favorite.

2	(4-ounce) trout fillets
¾	cup skim milk
¼	cup flour
¼	cup pumpkin seed kernels, toasted
½	teaspoon barbecue seasoning or Cajun seasoning
2	tablespoons pumpkin seed kernels, toasted

Soak the fillets in the skim milk in a shallow dish at room temperature for 15 minutes, turning once or twice. Process the flour, ¼ cup pumpkin seed kernels and barbecue seasoning in a food processor until fairly smooth.

Drain the fillets, discarding the skim milk. Coat the fillets with the flour mixture. Spray both sides of the fillets lightly with nonstick cooking spray. Arrange the fillets flesh side up on a baking rack sprayed with nonstick cooking spray. Place the rack on a baking sheet.

Bake at 425 degrees for 15 to 20 minutes or until the fillets flake easily, sprinkling each fillet with 1 tablespoon pumpkin seed kernels 2 minutes before the end of the baking process.

Tip: Pumpkin seeds are located with other nuts or snack foods in your local grocery store.

YIELD: 2 SERVINGS

Nutrients Per Serving: Cal 308; Prot 30 g; Carbo 23 g; T Fat 10 g; (Saturated Fat 2 g); Chol 66 mg; Fiber 1 g; Sod 318 mg
Nutritional information includes the entire amount of skim milk.

Fish Tacos

You will be surprised how easy these delicious tacos are to prepare.

CILANTRO SAUCE

½	cup reduced-fat ranch salad dressing
½	cup plain fat-free yogurt
½	cup trimmed fresh cilantro leaves
2	tablespoons chopped canned green chiles

TACOS

1	pound grilled any type white fish
2	cups shredded cabbage
1	avocado, cut into 8 slices
8	(6-inch) flour tortillas
	Juice of 1 lime

For the sauce, combine the salad dressing, yogurt, cilantro and chiles in a blender or food processor container. Process until smooth.

For the tacos, cut the fish into eight 2-ounce portions. Layer ¼ cup cabbage, 2 ounces fish and 1 slice of avocado on each tortilla. Fold over to enclose the filling. Top each taco with some of the sauce and drizzle with lime juice.

Tip: If time is of the essence, substitute frozen grilled fish fillets for the grilled white fish and coleslaw mix for the shredded cabbage.

YIELD: 8 TACOS

Nutrients Per Taco: Cal 341; Prot 19 g; Carbo 31 g; T Fat 15 g; (Saturated Fat 3 g); Chol 46 mg; Fiber 3 g; Sod 403 mg

When poaching fish, add lemon juice to the water to ensure that the fish retains that bright white color.

Balsamic-Glazed Tuna

⅓   cup chicken broth

1½   tablespoons balsamic vinegar

1½   tablespoons reduced-sodium soy sauce

2   tablespoons brown sugar

2¼   teaspoons cornstarch

4   (6-ounce) tuna steaks

1¼   teaspoons coarsely ground pepper

¼   teaspoon salt

¼   cup diagonally sliced green onions

Combine the broth, balsamic vinegar, soy sauce, brown sugar and cornstarch in a saucepan and mix well. Bring to a boil, stirring occasionally. Boil for 1 minute or until of glaze consistency, stirring constantly. Remove from heat. Cover to keep warm.

Sprinkle the tuna with the pepper and salt. Grill over medium-hot coals for 7 minutes per side or until the tuna flakes easily, turning once. Remove the tuna to a serving platter. Drizzle with the warm glaze. Sprinkle with the green onions.

YIELD: 4 SERVINGS

Nutrients Per Serving: Cal 297; Prot 42 g; Carbo 10 g; T Fat 9 g; (Saturated Fat 2 g); Chol 67 mg; Fiber <1 g; Sod 481 mg

Grilled Tuna with Strawberry Salsa

STRAWBERRY SALSA

1   pint fresh strawberries, coarsely chopped
4   green onions, chopped
2   teaspoons Dijon mustard
1   teaspoon orange zest
1   teaspoon red wine vinegar

TUNA

4   (6-ounce) tuna steaks
1   teaspoon canola oil
      salt and pepper to taste

For the salsa, combine the strawberries, green onions, Dijon mustard, orange zest and wine vinegar in a bowl and mix gently. Chill, covered, for 1 hour.

For the tuna, brush each side of the tuna lightly with the canola oil. Sprinkle with salt and pepper. Grill over medium-hot coals for 10 minutes or until the tuna flakes easily, turning once. Remove the tuna to a serving platter. Top each with ¼ of the salsa just before serving.

YIELD: 4 SERVINGS

Nutrients Per Serving: **Cal 290; Prot 42 g; Carbo 6 g; T Fat 10 g; (Saturated Fat 2 g); Chol 67 mg; Fiber 2 g; Sod 134 mg**

Although when we think of salsa we typically think of the traditional tomato salsa, salsa can be made from a variety of vegetables or fruits. It can add a refreshing combination of flavors that enhance even the blandest of foods.

Linguini with Red Clam Sauce

Simplicity with a fabulous aroma.

2	(6-ounce) cans chopped clams
12	ounces linguini
4	green onions, sliced
1	teaspoon olive oil
3	garlic cloves, minced
¼	teaspoon crushed red pepper
1	(14-ounce) can diced tomatoes
¼	cup dry white wine
2	teaspoons basil
1	teaspoon oregano
2	tablespoons grated Parmesan cheese

Drain the clams, reserving the liquid. Cook the linguini using package directions; drain. Cover to keep warm.

Sauté the green onions in the olive oil in a large nonstick skillet over medium heat for 2 to 3 minutes or until tender. Stir in the garlic and red pepper. Sauté for 1 minute longer. Add the reserved clam liquid, undrained tomatoes, white wine, basil and oregano and mix well. Bring to a boil; reduce heat.

Simmer for 10 to 12 minutes or until the liquid is reduced by ⅓, stirring frequently. Stir in the clams. Cook just until heated through, stirring frequently. Combine with the warm linguini in a serving bowl and toss to mix. Sprinkle with the cheese.

YIELD: 6 SERVINGS

Nutrients Per Serving: Cal 265; Prot 9 g; Carbo 49 g; T Fat 2 g; (Saturated Fat 1 g); Chol 3 mg; Fiber 3 g; Sod 277 mg

Shrimp and Scallop Kabobs

1	cup orange juice
½	cup rice vinegar
3	tablespoons chopped fresh basil
2	garlic cloves, minced
18	sea scallops
24	peeled large fresh shrimp with tails
18	mushrooms
18	cherry tomatoes
18	¼-inch slices yellow squash
18	1x1-inch pieces red bell pepper

Combine the orange juice, rice vinegar, basil and garlic in a 1-gallon sealable plastic bag. Add the scallops, shrimp, mushrooms, cherry tomatoes, yellow squash and red pepper and seal tightly. Toss to coat. Marinate in the refrigerator for 30 to 45 minutes, turning occasionally; drain.

Thread 3 scallops, 4 shrimp, 3 mushrooms, 3 cherry tomatoes, 3 slices yellow squash and 3 pieces red pepper on each of six 12-inch skewers, alternating the vegetables and seafood.

Arrange the kabobs on a baking sheet or broiler pan. Broil for 10 to 12 minutes or until the scallops are tender, the shrimp turn pink and the vegetables are tender-crisp, turning halfway through the cooking process.

YIELD: 6 SERVINGS

Nutrients Per Serving: Cal 186; Prot 24 g; Carbo 14 g; T Fat 4 g; (Saturated Fat 1 g); Chol 73 mg; Fiber 2 g; Sod 440 mg
Nutritional information includes the entire amount of marinade.

Most fish are low in fat, with white fish like cod, flounder, sole, and halibut being the lowest. Shellfish such as shrimp, lobster, clams, oysters, and mussels are also low in fat, but tend to be a bit higher in cholesterol. Don't overlook the fattier fish such as salmon, swordfish, and tuna. They are good sources of the beneficial omega-3 fatty acids.

Spicy Shrimp Paella

A versatile, low-fat recipe. You can easily add your favorite ingredients to create a signature dish.

4½   cups reduced-sodium chicken broth
3   ounces tomato paste
½   teaspoon whole thyme
¼   teaspoon paprika
¼   teaspoon black pepper
      cayenne pepper to taste
1   pound large shrimp, peeled, deveined
1   cup chopped onion
½   cup chopped red bell pepper
1   garlic clove, minced
2   teaspoons olive oil
1½   cups arborio rice

Combine the broth, tomato paste, thyme, paprika, black pepper and cayenne pepper in a medium saucepan and mix well. Bring to a boil. Add the shrimp. Boil until the shrimp turn pink, stirring occasionally. Remove the shrimp with a slotted spoon to a plate, reserving the liquid.

Sauté the onion, red pepper and garlic in the olive oil in a large nonstick skillet until the vegetables are tender. Add the rice and mix well. Cook until the rice is light brown, stirring constantly. Stir in 1 cup of the reserved liquid.

Cook over medium heat until the liquid is absorbed, stirring constantly. Stir in the remaining reserved liquid ½ cup at a time, cooking until the liquid has been absorbed after each addition and stirring constantly. This should take approximately 20 to 25 minutes. Stir in the shrimp. Cook just until heated through, stirring constantly. Serve immediately.

YIELD: 6 SERVINGS

Nutrients Per Serving: **Cal 318; Prot 17 g; Carbo 52 g; T Fat 3 g; (Saturated Fat 1 g); Chol 93 mg; Fiber 2 g; Sod 297 mg**

MEATLESS ENTREES

MEATLESS ENTREES

Black Bean Tortilla Casserole

1	cup chopped onion
2	cups chopped red and green bell peppers
2	garlic cloves, minced
2	(15-ounce) cans black beans, drained, rinsed
1	(14-ounce) can no-salt-added chopped tomatoes
1	cup picante sauce
1	tablespoon cumin
12	(6-inch) corn tortillas
1½	cups shredded reduced-fat Monterey Jack cheese
2	cups shredded lettuce
½	cup chopped tomato
⅓	cup reduced-fat sour cream

Sauté the onion in a large nonstick skillet coated with nonstick cooking spray until tender. Add the bell peppers and garlic and mix well. Sauté for 3 minutes longer or until the bell peppers are tender. Stir in the beans, undrained tomatoes, picante sauce and cumin. Cook for 5 minutes, stirring occasionally. Remove from heat.

Spread 1 cup of the bean mixture in a 9x13-inch baking pan sprayed with nonstick cooking spray. Arrange 6 of the tortillas in a single layer over the bean mixture. Spread with ¾ cup of the cheese. Spoon 2½ cups of the remaining bean mixture over the cheese. Top with the remaining 6 tortillas and spread with the remaining bean mixture.

Bake, covered, at 350 degrees for 30 minutes; remove cover. Sprinkle with the remaining ¾ cup cheese. Bake for 5 minutes longer or until the cheese melts. Let stand for 5 minutes before serving. Cut into 6 large portions. Top each portion with the shredded lettuce, tomato and sour cream.

YIELD: 6 SERVINGS

Nutrients Per Serving: Cal 389; Prot 22 g; Carbo 57 g; T Fat 9 g; (Saturated Fat 4 g); Chol 20 mg; Fiber 14 g; Sod 942 mg

Cowgirl Beans

1	teaspoon canola oil
2	cups chopped onions
1	tablespoon chopped jalapeño chiles
1	(14-ounce) can diced tomatoes
1	tablespoon catsup
½	cup chopped fresh cilantro
1	teaspoon (or less) salt
2	(15-ounce) cans pinto beans, drained, rinsed

Heat the canola oil in a large saucepan over medium heat. Add the onions and chiles. Sauté for 5 minutes. Stir in the undrained tomatoes, catsup, cilantro and salt. Simmer for 10 minutes, stirring occasionally.

Process 1 can of the undrained beans in a blender until puréed. Add the remaining can of undrained beans and puréed beans to the tomato mixture and mix well. Simmer for 15 minutes, stirring occasionally. Serve over hot cooked rice.

YIELD: 4 SERVINGS

Nutrients Per Serving: Cal 249; Prot 12 g; Carbo 45 g; T Fat 3 g; (Saturated Fat <1 g); Chol 0 mg; Fiber 12 g; Sod 1426 mg

Boulder Burritos

These make a great healthy grab-and-go meal, an adventurous way to add more greens to your diet.

1	cup water
½	cup bulgur
1	large onion, chopped
4	garlic cloves, minced
3	tablespoons olive oil
6	cups chopped kale
1	(15-ounce) can pinto beans, drained, rinsed
2	tablespoons lemon juice
2	teaspoons cumin
8	(10-inch) flour tortillas
1	cup salsa
1	cup shredded reduced-fat Cheddar cheese

Combine the water and bulgur in a saucepan and mix well. Simmer for 20 minutes or until tender.

Sauté the onion and garlic in the olive oil in a large skillet until the onion is tender. Stir in the kale. Sauté until wilted. Add the bulgur, beans, lemon juice and cumin and mix well. Cook just until heated through, stirring occasionally. Remove from heat.

Spoon ⅛ of the bean mixture on each tortilla. Top each with 2 tablespoons of the salsa and 2 tablespoons of the cheese. Roll to enclose the filling. Arrange seam side down in a 9x13-inch baking dish. Bake, covered, at 350 degrees for 15 minutes or until heated through or microwave on Medium for 3 to 4 minutes.

YIELD: 8 BURRITOS

Nutrients Per Burrito: Cal 423; Prot 16 g; Carbo 64 g; T Fat 12 g; (Saturated Fat 3 g); Chol 3 mg; Fiber 8 g; Sod 751 mg

Sesame Chick-Pea Dinner Wraps

2	tablespoons sesame seeds
1	(15-ounce) can chick-peas, drained, rinsed
6	cups slivered romaine
1	red bell pepper, finely chopped
4	ounces reduced-fat feta cheese, crumbled
3	tablespoons lemon juice
1	tablespoon olive oil
1	tablespoon chopped fresh basil, or 1 teaspoon dried basil
1	teaspoon minced garlic
½	teaspoon freshly ground pepper
6	(10-inch) flour tortillas, heated

Toast the sesame seeds in an ungreased skillet over medium heat until golden brown and fragrant, stirring frequently. Process the chick-peas in a blender or food processor until coarsely chopped.

Toss the romaine and red pepper in a salad bowl. Add the feta cheese and chick-peas and mix well. Sprinkle with the sesame seeds. Whisk the lemon juice, olive oil, basil, garlic and pepper in a bowl. Drizzle over the romaine mixture, tossing to coat. Spoon 1 cup of the romaine mixture in the center of each tortilla. Roll to enclose the filling.

YIELD: 6 WRAPS

Nutrients Per Wrap: Cal 423; Prot 14 g; Carbo 61 g; T Fat 14 g; (Saturated Fat 5 g); Chol 17 mg; Fiber 7 g; Sod 773 mg

Sesame seeds and olive oil are good sources of monounsaturated fats, which help lower blood cholesterol levels.

Portobello Florentine

4	whole portobello mushrooms, stems and black "ribs" removed
½	teaspoon olive oil
1	(10-ounce) package frozen chopped spinach, thawed, drained
¼	cup chopped onion
3	tablespoons dry bread crumbs
2	teaspoons grated Parmesan cheese
1	teaspoon garlic powder
1	teaspoon oregano
1	egg, lightly beaten
¼	cup shredded mozzarella cheese

Arrange the mushrooms top side down on a baking sheet. Heat the olive oil in a large nonstick skillet over medium heat. Add the spinach and onion and mix well.

Sauté for 10 minutes or until the onion is tender. Stir in the bread crumbs, Parmesan cheese, garlic powder and oregano. Remove from heat. Stir in the egg.

Spoon equal portions of the spinach mixture onto each mushroom and pat firmly. Top each with 1 tablespoon of the mozzarella cheese. Bake at 375 degrees for 15 to 20 minutes or until light brown.

YIELD: 4 SERVINGS

Nutrients Per Serving: **Cal 139; Prot 14 g; Carbo 18 g; T Fat 4 g; (Saturated Fat 2 g); Chol 59 mg; Fiber 10 g; Sod 183 mg**

Mushrooms can add a meaty texture to a dish without adding extra fat grams. Here are some tips for making the most of mushrooms:
*
Choose blemish-free mushrooms with a smooth, dry surface.
*
Store mushrooms unrinsed in the refrigerator in a paper bag. Plastic bags will cause mushrooms to spoil.
*
To clean mushrooms, fill a plastic bag with water. Add the mushrooms, quickly swirl to loosen the dirt, and drain.

Portobello Mushroom Stir-Fry

This recipe was contributed by Marty Meitus, the Food Editor of the Denver Rocky Mountain News.

1	teaspoon canola oil
1	small onion, chopped
1	red bell pepper, julienned
6	ounces portobello mushrooms, sliced
2	tablespoons balsamic vinegar
1	teaspoon reduced-sodium soy sauce
1	teaspoon Worcestershire sauce
4	cups cooked brown rice

Heat the canola oil in a large skillet over medium-high heat. Add the onion and red pepper. Stir-fry for 2 to 3 minutes. Add the mushrooms.

Stir-fry until the vegetables are tender. Stir in the balsamic vinegar, soy sauce and Worcestershire sauce. Cook over low heat until most of the liquid is absorbed. Spoon over the brown rice on a serving platter.

YIELD: 4 SERVINGS

Nutrients Per Serving: Cal 259; Prot 7 g; Carbo 52 g; T Fat 3 g; (Saturated Fat <1 g); Chol 0 mg; Fiber 6 g; Sod 74 mg

Roasting peppers is easy, done individually or in quantity, and they may be frozen for future use. To roast a single pepper, use your stove top burner. Secure the pepper with a long-handled fork or skewer. Turn the burner to high and rotate the pepper until it is evenly charred on all sides. Place the pepper in a paper bag and seal tightly. Let stand until cool. Remove the charred skin. →

Grilled Portobello Mushroom Sandwiches

½   cup balsamic vinegar
¼   cup Worcestershire sauce
2   green onions, finely chopped
1   tablespoon olive oil
1   teaspoon rosemary, crushed
4   portobello mushrooms, stems removed
4   Kaiser rolls, split
2   ounces goat or feta cheese, crumbled
⅓   cup chopped roasted red bell pepper
1   cup fresh spinach leaves

Combine the balsamic vinegar, Worcestershire sauce, green onions, olive oil and rosemary in a sealable plastic bag. Add the mushrooms and seal tightly. Toss to coat. Marinate at room temperature for 20 to 30 minutes, turning occasionally; drain.

Grill the mushrooms over medium-high heat for 4 to 6 minutes per side or until tender. Place the rolls cut side down on the grill rack. Grill for 2 to 3 minutes or until light brown; watch carefully.

Layer the cheese, mushroom caps, red pepper and spinach in the order listed on the bottom roll halves. Top with the remaining roll halves. Serve with a salad of mixed salad greens.

Tip: Do not forget that roasted red and yellow bell peppers are commercially available in most supermarkets or in some supermarket delis. They can be used when fresh bell peppers are not available or are too expensive.

YIELD: 4 SANDWICHES

Nutrients Per Sandwich: Cal 410; Prot 18 g; Carbo 58 g; T Fat 13 g; (Saturated Fat 5 g); Chol 15 mg; Fiber 8 g; Sod 856 mg
Nutritional information includes the entire amount of marinade.

To roast several peppers, rinse the peppers and pierce with a fork or sharp knife. Arrange the peppers in a single layer on a baking sheet. Broil until they are evenly charred on all sides, turning frequently. Proceed as above. Or grill the peppers over hot coals until charred and blistered. As you can see, you have several options when roasting peppers.

Layered Rigatoni Bake

1¾ cups rigatoni
1 pound firm tofu, mashed
¼ cup grated fat-free Parmesan cheese
1 teaspoon Italian spice blend
½ teaspoon garlic powder
½ teaspoon onion powder
1 (25-ounce) jar chunky vegetable pasta sauce
1 cup shredded mozzarella cheese

Cook the pasta using package directions until al dente. Drain and rinse. Combine the tofu, Parmesan cheese, Italian spice blend, garlic powder and onion powder in a bowl and mix well.

Layer the pasta sauce, pasta, tofu mixture and mozzarella cheese ½ at a time in a 2-quart baking dish sprayed with nonstick cooking spray. Bake at 350 degrees for 20 minutes.

YIELD: 4 SERVINGS

Nutrients Per Serving: Cal 366; Prot 24 g; Carbo 44 g; T Fat 10 g; (Saturated Fat 4 g); Chol 22 mg; Fiber 4 g; Sod 808 mg

Long-Life Noodles

A fabulous meal for an office party or family gathering. Assign a topping to each guest and the work is light. The long noodles symbolize long life!

PEANUT SAUCE

1/4	cup each smooth peanut butter and hot water
3	garlic cloves, minced
3	green onions, sliced
2	tablespoons each reduced-sodium soy sauce and red wine vinegar
1	tablespoon each canola oil and sugar
1/4	teaspoon cayenne pepper

TOPPINGS AND PASTA

5	ounces snow peas
1	cucumber, cut into quarters, seeded (optional)
3	eggs, beaten
2	cups fresh bean sprouts
2	cups julienned fresh spinach (optional)
2	large carrots, shredded
4	green onions, diagonally sliced
18	ounces fresh linguini, cooked, chilled

For the sauce, combine the peanut butter, hot water, garlic, green onions, soy sauce, wine vinegar, canola oil, sugar and cayenne pepper in a blender or food processor container. Process until smooth.

For the toppings, steam the snow peas in a steamer until tender; drain. Slice the snow peas lengthwise into thin strips. Cut the cucumber crosswise into 1/4-inch slices.

Spray a small nonstick skillet with nonstick cooking spray. Pour the eggs into the prepared skillet, tilting to cover the bottom to form a thin pancake. Cook over medium heat until firm, turning once; do not stir. Invert onto a plate. Cut the egg pancake into thin strips.

To assemble, arrange the snow peas, cucumber, egg strips, bean sprouts, spinach, carrots and green onions on a serving platter. Spoon the pasta into a serving bowl. Everyone helps themselves to a portion of the pasta, adds the desired toppings and drizzles with the sauce.

YIELD: 8 SERVINGS

Nutrients Per Serving: Cal 386; Prot 15 g; Carbo 61 g; T Fat 9 g; (Saturated Fat 2 g); Chol 80 mg; Fiber 6 g; Sod 202 mg

Spiced Lentils over Pasta

½	cup brown lentils
8	ounces pasta
1	small onion, finely chopped
3	garlic cloves, minced
1	tablespoon canola oil
1	teaspoon cumin
1	teaspoon ground ginger
½	teaspoon red pepper flakes
1	(16-ounce) can diced tomatoes
1¼	cups vegetable broth or water
1	tablespoon sugar
½	cup plain fat-free yogurt
2	tablespoons finely shredded fresh basil

Sort and rinse the lentils. Cook the pasta using package directions; drain. Cover to keep warm.

Sauté the onion and garlic in the canola oil in a saucepan for 5 minutes or until the onion is tender. Stir in the cumin, ginger and red pepper flakes. Sauté for 1 minute longer. Add the lentils, undrained tomatoes, broth and sugar and mix well.

Simmer for 20 to 25 minutes or until the lentils are tender, stirring occasionally. Remove from heat. Stir in the yogurt and basil. Spoon over the pasta on a serving platter.

YIELD: 4 SERVINGS

Nutrients Per Serving: **Cal 389; Prot 22 g; Carbo 65 g; T Fat 5 g; (Saturated Fat <1 g); Chol 1 mg; Fiber 10 g; Sod 531 mg**

Listed below are a few tips on how to plan meatless meals.
*
Center meals around the entrées that are not typically thought of as vegetarian, such as soups and sandwiches, pasta with marinara sauce, macaroni and cheese, vegetable "fried" rice, or bean burritos.
*
Do not worry about protein. If you are getting sufficient calories and your diet is varied, protein requirements are easily met. →

Spinach Quesadillas

1	(10-ounce) package frozen chopped spinach
2	tablespoons minced onion
2	tablespoons minced garlic
2	tablespoons minced mushrooms
2	tablespoons minced fresh jalapeño chiles
2	tablespoons minced fresh cilantro
8	(6-inch) corn tortillas
4	ounces fat-free refried beans
¼	cup shredded mozzarella cheese

 Combine the spinach with a small amount of water in a microwave-safe dish. Microwave, covered, on High for 5 minutes or until the spinach is thawed; drain. Squeeze the excess moisture from the spinach. Combine the spinach, onion, garlic, mushrooms, chiles and cilantro in a bowl and mix well.

Arrange 4 of the tortillas in a single layer on a baking sheet sprayed with nonstick cooking spray. Spread the tortillas with the refried beans. Spread with the spinach mixture and sprinkle with the cheese. Top with the remaining tortillas. Bake at 375 degrees for 15 to 20 minutes or until light brown. Serve with salsa.

YIELD: 4 QUESADILLAS

Nutrients Per Quesadilla: Cal 200; Prot 9 g; Carbo 37 g; T Fat 3 g; (Saturated Fat 1 g); Chol 6 mg; Fiber 7 g; Sod 274 mg

*
High-protein foods such as cheese, beans, or meat substitutes are not necessary at every meal.
*
Vegetarians do not need to worry about eating special combinations of foods to meet protein requirements.
*
Be aware of the fat content of the servings; a vegetarian diet can still be high in fat if you use too many nuts, oils, full-fat tofu or soy products, or too many sweets.

Tempeh is a flat cake made from fermented soybeans. Unlike tofu, which takes on the flavors of the foods with which it is cooked, tempeh has a smoky flavor and a chewy texture. Here are some suggestions for preparation: grill tempeh after marinating in a sauce of your choice; chop tempeh and mix in casseroles, chili, or soups; grill and top with "burger fixings."

Cranberry-Glazed Tempeh

If you like tempeh, you will love this recipe.

2	(8-ounce) packages wild rice tempeh
1	(15-ounce) can whole cranberry sauce
½	cup water
2	tablespoons maple syrup
1	tablespoon soy sauce
1	tablespoon dry sherry
1	tablespoon grated fresh gingerroot
¼	teaspoon allspice
¼	teaspoon cinnamon
¼	teaspoon salt
⅛	teaspoon nutmeg
	cayenne pepper to taste

Cut each block of tempeh into 4 triangles. Steam the tempeh in a steamer basket for 10 minutes. Arrange in a single layer in a baking dish.

Combine the cranberry sauce, water, maple syrup, soy sauce, sherry, gingerroot, allspice, cinnamon, salt, nutmeg and cayenne pepper in a blender or food processor container. Process until smooth. Pour over the tempeh. Bake at 350 degrees for 40 to 45 minutes.

YIELD: 4 SERVINGS

Nutrients Per Serving: Cal 409; Prot 22 g; Carbo 66 g; T Fat 9 g; (Saturated Fat 1 g); Chol 0 mg; Fiber 8 g; Sod 505 mg

Grilled Tofu Steaks

1	pound firm tofu, cut lengthwise into 4 steaks
1/4	cup reduced-sodium soy sauce
1/4	cup red wine vinegar
1	teaspoon olive oil
1	teaspoon sesame oil
1/2	teaspoon oregano
1/4	teaspoon garlic powder
1/8	teaspoon ginger powder
	pepper to taste

Place the tofu on a plate lined with paper towels. Cover the tofu with additional paper towels. Top with a plate. Weight with several canned goods or a cast-iron skillet to press out the excess moisture. Let stand for 20 minutes.

Combine the soy sauce, wine vinegar, olive oil, sesame oil, oregano, garlic powder, ginger and pepper in a shallow dish and mix well. Add the tofu steaks, turning to coat. Marinate, covered, in the refrigerator for 6 hours or longer, turning once; drain. Grill over medium-hot coals for 6 minutes per side or until brown. May broil if desired.

YIELD: 4 SERVINGS

Nutrients Per Serving: Cal 110; Prot 9 g; Carbo 5 g; T Fat 5 g;
(Saturated Fat 1 g); Chol 0 mg; Fiber <1 g; Sod 547 mg
Nutritional information includes the entire amount of marinade.

Telluride Tofu and Mushrooms

Mushrooms provide a meaty texture for this vegetarian dish.

1	pound firm tofu, cut into ½-inch slices
½	cup reduced-sodium soy sauce
1	tablespoon brown sugar
1	tablespoon olive oil
2	cups sliced fresh mushrooms
2	garlic cloves, minced
1	large tomato, chopped
¼	cup chopped green onions
4	cups hot cooked rice

 Place the tofu on a plate lined with paper towels. Cover the tofu with additional paper towels. Top with a plate. Weight with several canned goods or a cast-iron skillet to press out the excess moisture. Pressing the moisture out of the tofu allows it to become firm and absorb the sauce.

Combine the soy sauce and brown sugar in a small bowl and mix well. Heat the olive oil in a large nonstick skillet. Add the mushrooms and garlic. Sauté over medium heat until the mushrooms are tender.

Cut the tofu into ½-inch cubes. Stir into the mushroom mixture. Add the soy sauce mixture, tomato and green onions and mix well. Cook for 5 minutes, stirring frequently. Spoon over the rice on a serving platter.

YIELD: 4 SERVINGS

Nutrients Per Serving: **Cal 370; Prot 16 g; Carbo 60 g; T Fat 7 g; (Saturated Fat 1 g); Chol 0 mg; Fiber 2 g; Sod 1061 mg**

*H*ere are a few helpful hints to make cooking with tofu easy:
*
Use silken tofu with its smooth creamy texture for dressings, dips, and desserts. Stir into sauces, use in the place of cream in Alfredo sauce or instead of sour cream or mayonnaise in recipes, or use it to make pie fillings, custards, or cheesecakes. →

Vegetable Tofu Curry

3	cups water
3	potatoes, peeled, cubed
3	carrots, cut into 1/4-inch slices
1	teaspoon salt
1 1/2	tablespoons canola oil
1	large onion, chopped
1	large apple, sliced
1/3	cup raisins
8	ounces firm tofu, cubed
3	tablespoons unbleached white flour
2	tablespoons curry powder
1 1/2	teaspoons cinnamon
2	teaspoons reduced-sodium soy sauce

Bring the water to a boil in a 4-quart saucepan. Add the potatoes, carrots and salt. Cook for 15 minutes or until the vegetables are tender. Drain, reserving the vegetable broth. Return the vegetables to the saucepan. Cover to keep warm.

Heat the canola oil in a large skillet over medium-high heat. Add the onion. Sauté for 5 minutes or until tender; reduce heat. Stir in the apple and raisins. Cook over low heat for 10 minutes, stirring occasionally. Add the tofu and mix well.

Cook for 5 minutes, stirring frequently. Sprinkle the flour, curry powder and cinnamon over the tofu mixture and mix well. Stir in the reserved vegetable broth and soy sauce.

Cook until thickened, stirring constantly. Add to the potatoes and carrots and mix gently. Serve over hot cooked basmati rice with chutney on the side.

YIELD: 5 SERVINGS

Nutrients Per Serving: Cal 227; Prot 7 g; Carbo 39 g; T Fat 6 g; (Saturated Fat 1 g); Chol 0 mg; Fiber 5 g; Sod 572 mg

*

Soft tofu is moist and a bit firmer and can also be used for dressings and dips. Use as a substitution for soft cheeses such as ricotta.

*

Firm and extra-firm tofu holds its texture and shape and is best in salads, stir-fry, and in recipes that call for meat or chicken.

Vegetable Barley Bake

1	(15-ounce) can black beans, drained, rinsed
1	(10-ounce) package frozen whole kernel corn, thawed
1¼	cups vegetable broth
1	cup quartered fresh mushrooms
½	cup pearl barley
¼	cup bulgur
2	medium carrots, peeled, thinly sliced
¼	cup chopped onion
1	garlic clove, minced
½	cup shredded sharp Cheddar cheese

Combine the beans, corn, broth, mushrooms, barley, bulgur, carrots, onion and garlic in a bowl and mix gently. Spoon into a baking dish.

Bake, covered, at 350 degrees for 1 hour, stirring halfway through the cooking process. Sprinkle with the cheese. Let stand, covered, for 5 minutes or until the cheese melts. Serve immediately.

YIELD: 4 SERVINGS

Nutrients Per Serving: Cal 350; Prot 16 g; Carbo 61 g; T Fat 7 g; (Saturated Fat 3 g); Chol 15 mg; Fiber 14 g; Sod 747 mg

VEGETABLES
GRAINS
AND PASTA

VEGETABLES, GRAINS AND PASTA

Roasted Artichokes

3	cups cold water
	juice of 1 large lemon
4	artichokes
½	cup dry white wine
2	teaspoons thyme, crushed
1	teaspoon olive oil
	salt and pepper to taste
2	bay leaves, torn into halves

Combine the cold water and lemon juice in a large bowl. Trim the artichokes by clipping the thorns off the tips of the leaves. Slice approximately 1 inch off the top of each artichoke. Cut off the stem at the base of each artichoke. Cut the artichokes into sixths. Add to the lemon juice mixture immediately.

Whisk the white wine, thyme, olive oil, salt and pepper in a bowl. Remove the artichokes from the lemon juice mixture and pat dry with paper towels. Add the artichokes to the white wine mixture, tossing to coat. Arrange in a single layer in a baking dish sprayed with nonstick cooking spray. Drizzle with any remaining white wine mixture. Place the bay leaves between the artichokes. Cover with waxed paper and then with foil.

Bake at 400 degrees for 30 minutes; remove cover. Bake for 20 minutes longer or until crisp around the edges and just beginning to brown. Discard the bay leaves. Serve with fat-free ranch salad dressing.

YIELD: 4 SERVINGS

Nutrients Per Serving: Cal 94; Prot 4 g; Carbo 15 g; T Fat 1 g; (Saturated Fat <1 g); Chol 0 mg; Fiber 7 g; Sod 122 mg

Vegetables are full of beneficial compounds called phytochemicals; researchers suspect there are hundreds of them. They are believed to have powerful antioxidant properties, helping to reduce the risk of certain types of cancer and heart disease.

Awesome Asparagus

An easy way to dress up asparagus.

1	pound fresh asparagus, trimmed
1½	tablespoons butter, melted
2	teaspoons balsamic vinegar
1	tablespoon pine nuts or other chopped nuts, toasted

Steam the asparagus in a steamer until tender-crisp; drain. Arrange on a serving platter. Whisk the butter and balsamic vinegar in a bowl. Drizzle over the asparagus. Sprinkle with the pine nuts.

YIELD: 4 SERVINGS

Nutrients Per Serving: **Cal 78; Prot 3 g; Carbo 6 g; T Fat 6 g; (Saturated Fat 3 g); Chol 12 mg; Fiber 2 g; Sod 47 mg**

Broccoli Dijon

1	tablespoon Dijon mustard
1	tablespoon reduced-sodium soy sauce
1	tablespoon white wine vinegar
1	teaspoon canola oil
2	cups broccoli florets

Whisk the Dijon mustard, soy sauce, wine vinegar and canola oil in a bowl. Steam the broccoli in a steamer until tender-crisp; drain.
Arrange the broccoli on a serving platter. Drizzle with the mustard mixture. Serve immediately.

YIELD: 4 SERVINGS

Nutrients Per Serving: **Cal 30; Prot 2 g; Carbo 3 g; T Fat 2 g; (Saturated Fat <1 g); Chol 0 mg; Fiber 1 g; Sod 231 mg**

Balsamic vinegar, once an obscure condiment in Italy, has now become a popular ingredient in reduced-fat recipes. Balsamic vinegar is less acidic than most vinegars and adds a gentle sweetness to any dish.

Maple-Glazed Carrots

1	pound baby carrots, julienned
1	tablespoon lemon juice
1	tablespoon maple syrup
1	teaspoon butter
1/8	teaspoon cinnamon
	salt and pepper to taste

Steam the carrots in a steamer for 4 to 6 minutes or until tender-crisp; drain. Cover to keep warm.

Combine the lemon juice, maple syrup, butter, cinnamon, salt and pepper in a saucepan. Cook just until the butter melts, stirring occasionally. Add the carrots, tossing to coat. Serve immediately.

YIELD: 6 SERVINGS

Nutrients Per Serving: Cal 44; Prot 1 g; Carbo 9 g; T Fat 1 g; (Saturated Fat <1 g); Chol 2 mg; Fiber 1 g; Sod 33 mg

Steam or microwave vegetables in as little water as possible. Both vitamins and minerals can seep into the cooking water and be lost when drained. If you have to use a considerable amount of water, as when boiling potatoes, save the cooking water to make soups or sauces in the future.

Cauliflower in Spicy Tomato Sauce

1	(14-ounce) can diced tomatoes
1	cup chopped onion
2	garlic cloves, chopped
½	cup water
2	teaspoons balsamic vinegar
¾	teaspoon cumin
⅛	teaspoon white pepper
	cayenne pepper to taste
	florets of 1 head cauliflower
2	tablespoons chopped fresh parsley

 Combine the undrained tomatoes, onion and garlic in a food processor container. Process until smooth. Pour into a saucepan. Stir in the water, balsamic vinegar, cumin, white pepper and cayenne pepper.

Bring the tomato mixture to a boil; reduce heat. Simmer for 5 minutes, stirring occasionally. Add the cauliflower and mix gently. Simmer, covered, for 10 minutes or until the cauliflower is tender, stirring occasionally. Spoon into a serving bowl. Sprinkle with the parsley.

YIELD: 4 SERVINGS

Nutrients Per Serving: Cal 77; Prot 4 g; Carbo 16 g; T Fat <1 g; (Saturated Fat <1 g); Chol 0 mg; Fiber 5 g; Sod 217 mg

For a rich-tasting sauce, purée cooked vegetables with a little stock. This purée may be added to soups to increase their nutritional value as well as for added flavor.

Stuffed Eggplant Mediterranean-Style

1   small eggplant
1   teaspoon olive oil
¼   cup chopped onion
¼   cup chopped mushrooms
1   tomato, chopped
½   cup cooked rice
    salt and pepper to taste
¼   cup shredded mozzarella cheese

Cut the eggplant lengthwise into halves. Scoop out the pulp, leaving a ½-inch shell. Chop the eggplant pulp. Arrange the shells in an 8x8-inch baking dish sprayed with nonstick cooking spray.

Heat the olive oil in an 8-inch skillet. Add the eggplant, onion and mushrooms. Sauté for 5 minutes. Stir in the tomato. Cook for 5 to 10 minutes, stirring frequently. Add the rice, salt and pepper and mix well.

Spoon the eggplant mixture into the shells. Sprinkle with the cheese. Bake at 350 degrees for 35 to 40 minutes or until light brown.

YIELD: 2 SERVINGS

Nutrients Per Serving: Cal 187; Prot 7 g; Carbo 29 g; T Fat 6 g; (Saturated Fat 2 g); Chol 11 mg; Fiber 6 g; Sod 66 mg

Potatoes in Wine

1	pound unpeeled new potatoes, cut into ½-inch cubes
1	cup dry white wine
¼	cup white wine vinegar
2	green onions, thinly sliced
1	garlic clove, minced
½	teaspoon basil
⅛	teaspoon pepper
1	teaspoon Dijon mustard
1	tablespoon chopped fresh basil or parsley

Combine the potatoes, white wine, wine vinegar, green onions, garlic, basil and pepper in a saucepan. Bring to a boil; reduce heat. Simmer for 25 minutes or until the potatoes are tender. Remove the potatoes with a slotted spoon to a serving bowl, reserving the liquid. Cover the potatoes to keep warm.

Cook the reserved liquid until reduced and thickened, stirring occasionally. Stir in the Dijon mustard. Drizzle over the potatoes. Sprinkle with the basil. Serve immediately.

YIELD: 4 SERVINGS

Nutrients Per Serving: Cal 150; Prot 2 g; Carbo 25 g; T Fat <1 g; (Saturated Fat <1 g); Chol 0 mg; Fiber 2 g; Sod 44 mg

Mountain Mashers

This light version of garlic mashed potatoes is so flavorful you will never miss the gravy.

1½   pounds unpeeled red potatoes, cut into 1-inch cubes
2   tablespoons butter
1   tablespoon minced garlic
½   cup skim milk
1   teaspoon prepared horseradish
      salt and pepper to taste

Combine the red potatoes with enough water to cover in a saucepan. Bring to a boil; reduce heat. Simmer for 30 minutes or until tender; drain.

Heat the butter in a saucepan over medium heat until melted. Add the garlic. Sauté until light brown. Stir in the skim milk. Cook over low heat just until warm, stirring constantly. Stir in the horseradish. Remove from heat.

Beat the potatoes in a mixer bowl just until mashed. Add the skim milk mixture and beat until blended. Season with salt and pepper. The potatoes should be slightly lumpy.

YIELD: 6 SERVINGS

Nutrients Per Serving: Cal 146; Prot 3 g; Carbo 25 g; T Fat 4 g; (Saturated Fat 2 g); Chol 11 mg; Fiber 2 g; Sod 60 mg

Rosemary Potatoes

A great side dish that can be cooked in foil packets over an open campfire.

2	green onions, finely chopped
1	tablespoon olive oil
1	teaspoon rosemary, crushed
½	teaspoon garlic salt
2	pounds unpeeled red potatoes, cut into ½-inch cubes

Combine the green onions, olive oil, rosemary and garlic salt in a bowl. Add the red potatoes, tossing to coat. Spread the potatoes in a 9x13-inch baking pan. Bake, covered with foil, at 400 degrees for 25 to 30 minutes or until brown and tender.

YIELD: 6 SERVINGS

Nutrients Per Serving: Cal 155; Prot 3 g; Carbo 31 g; T Fat 2 g; (Saturated Fat <1 g); Chol 0 mg; Fiber 3 g; Sod 161 mg

Keep the skin intact on fruits and vegetables as much as possible. Peeling removes nutrients concentrated just under the skin and takes away valuable fiber.

Roasted Root Vegetables

Your family and guests will love the flavor and they will have fun identifying the vegetables.

2	pounds celery root or celeriac
1	pound rutabaga
1	pound baby carrots
1	tablespoon olive oil
1	large red onion, cut into 1-inch pieces
1	teaspoon ground sage
1	teaspoon salt

Peel the celery root. Cut into ½x2-inch strips. Peel the rutabaga. Cut into ½x2-inch strips. Combine the celery root, rutabaga, carrots and olive oil in a bowl, tossing to coat. Spoon the vegetable mixture into a shallow baking dish.

Roast at 400 degrees for 25 minutes. Stir in the red onion, sage and salt. Roast for 20 to 30 minutes longer or until the vegetables are tender and golden brown, stirring occasionally.

YIELD: 8 SERVINGS

Nutrients Per Serving: **Cal 111; Prot 3 g; Carbo 21 g; T Fat 2 g; (Saturated Fat <1 g); Chol 0 mg; Fiber 5 g; Sod 436 mg**

Be adventurous and try a vegetable you have not tasted before. Make it a monthly goal.

Sautéed Spinach with Corn Relish

CORN RELISH

1	cup frozen whole kernel corn, thawed
¼	cup chopped red bell pepper
3	tablespoons vinegar
2	tablespoons minced onion
1	tablespoon sugar

SPINACH

1	teaspoon olive oil
1	garlic clove, minced
10	ounces fresh spinach, trimmed

For the relish, combine the corn, red pepper, vinegar, onion and sugar in a bowl and mix well.

For the spinach, heat the olive oil in a large nonstick skillet. Add the garlic. Sauté for 2 minutes. Add the spinach. Sauté for 5 to 7 minutes or until the spinach is heated through and slightly wilted. Spoon into a serving bowl. Top with the relish.

Tip: The Corn Relish is also great served as a topping for pork or chicken or as a side dish.

YIELD: 4 SERVINGS

Nutrients Per Serving: Cal 81; Prot 3 g; Carbo 16 g; T Fat 2 g; (Saturated Fat <1 g); Chol 0 mg; Fiber 3 g; Sod 42 mg

Summer Squash and Mushroom Bake

1	small zucchini, cut into ½-inch chunks
1	small yellow squash, cut into ½-inch chunks
5	to 10 mushrooms, sliced (about 2 cups)
¼	cup thinly sliced red onion
½	cup shredded mozzarella cheese
2	tablespoons chopped fresh basil, or 1 tablespoon dried basil

Combine the zucchini, yellow squash, mushrooms and red onion in a 2-quart baking dish and mix well. Sprinkle with the cheese and basil.

Bake, covered, at 350 degrees for 25 to 30 minutes or until the vegetables are of the desired degree of crispness.

YIELD: 4 SERVINGS

Nutrients Per Serving: Cal 65; Prot 5 g; Carbo 5 g; T Fat 3 g; (Saturated Fat 2 g); Chol 11 mg; Fiber 2 g; Sod 54 mg

The flavor of fresh herbs can diminish with prolonged cooking, so it is best to add fresh herbs during the last twenty minutes of the cooking or baking process. On the other hand, if you are using fresh herbs in salad dressings, marinades, or other uncooked foods, add them at the beginning so that their flavor will have time to infuse the liquid.

Praline Sweet Potato Casserole

1	(16-ounce) can sweet potatoes, drained
1	egg, beaten
2	tablespoons sugar
¼	teaspoon vanilla extract
⅓	cup packed dark brown sugar
2	tablespoons chopped pecans
2	tablespoons flour
2	teaspoons margarine, melted

Mash the sweet potatoes in a bowl. Stir in the egg, sugar and vanilla. Spoon into a greased 2-quart shallow baking dish.

Combine the brown sugar, pecans, flour and margarine in a bowl and mix well. Add additional flour if the mixture is not crumbly. Sprinkle over the prepared layer. Bake at 350 degrees for 25 to 30 minutes or until light brown. Cover with foil as soon as the sweet potatoes begin to bubble to prevent the pecans from burning. May substitute 1 pound mashed baked fresh sweet potatoes for the canned sweet potatoes.

YIELD: 4 SERVINGS

Nutrients Per Serving: Cal 271; Prot 4 g; Carbo 52 g; T Fat 6 g; (Saturated Fat 1 g); Chol 53 mg; Fiber 2 g; Sod 105 mg

Got a nutrition question? Call your nearest registered dietitian or the Colorado Dietetic Association. You can also visit our web site at www.eatrightcolorado.org.

Washington Park Sweet Potatoes with Tart Cherries

This delicious sweet potato dish was adapted from a recipe served at the Washington Park Grille.

½	cup dried sour cherries
3	medium sweet potatoes, peeled, cut into ½-inch cubes
2	pears, peeled, cut into ½-inch cubes
2	Granny Smith apples, peeled, cut into ½-inch cubes
3	tablespoons honey
1	tablespoon olive oil
¾	teaspoon cinnamon
½	teaspoon nutmeg
	salt and pepper to taste

Pour enough hot water to cover over the cherries in a bowl. Let stand for 2 minutes; drain. Combine the cherries, sweet potatoes, pears and apples in a bowl and mix well. Spoon into a 9x13-inch baking pan.

Combine the honey, olive oil, cinnamon, nutmeg, salt and pepper in a microwave-safe bowl and mix well. Microwave on Medium for 30 seconds and stir. Pour over the sweet potato mixture, stirring to coat. Bake at 400 degrees for 30 to 40 minutes or until the sweet potatoes are tender.

YIELD: 8 SERVINGS

Nutrients Per Serving: Cal 161; Prot 2 g; Carbo 37 g; T Fat 2 g;
(Saturated Fat <1 g); Chol 0 mg; Fiber 3 g; Sod 6 mg

Sweet Potato Chips

3	medium sweet potatoes, peeled
2	teaspoons olive oil
1	teaspoon water
2	teaspoons cumin
1	teaspoon chili powder
½	teaspoon salt

Cut the sweet potatoes into ¼-inch slices. Place in a large sealable plastic bag. Pour a mixture of the olive oil and water over the sweet potatoes and seal tightly. Shake to coat.

Arrange the sweet potatoes in a single layer on a baking sheet. Sprinkle with a mixture of the cumin, chili powder and salt. Bake at 400 degrees for 20 to 25 minutes or until slightly crisp. Serve immediately.

Tip: Try using a crinkle-cut garnishing tool to slice the sweet potatoes.

YIELD: 4 SERVINGS

Nutrients Per Serving: Cal 110; Prot 2 g; Carbo 21 g; T Fat 2 g; (Saturated Fat <1 g); Chol 0 mg; Fiber 3 g; Sod 306 mg

Crispy Zucchini Coins

½	cup seasoned bread crumbs
3	tablespoons grated Parmesan cheese
¼	teaspoon pepper
3	cups thinly sliced zucchini
2	egg whites, lightly beaten

Combine the bread crumbs, cheese and pepper in a shallow dish and mix well. Dip the zucchini slices in the egg whites and coat with the bread crumb mixture.

Arrange the zucchini in a single layer on a baking sheet coated with nonstick cooking spray. Bake at 450 degrees for 20 minutes; turn. Bake for 15 minutes longer or until brown and crispy.

YIELD: 4 SERVINGS

Nutrients Per Serving: Cal 98; Prot 7 g; Carbo 14 g; T Fat 2 g; (Saturated Fat 1 g); Chol 4 mg; Fiber 2 g; Sod 515 mg

Fire-Grilled Vegetables

1	large green bell pepper
1	large red bell pepper
1	medium yellow squash, cut into ¼-inch slices
1	medium zucchini, cut into ¼-inch slices
¼	cup reduced-fat Italian salad dressing
1	tablespoon balsamic vinegar
1	tablespoon chopped fresh basil, or 1 teaspoon dried basil

Cut the bell peppers lengthwise into quarters. Combine the bell peppers, yellow squash and zucchini in a bowl and mix gently.

Whisk the salad dressing, balsamic vinegar and basil in a bowl. Pour over the vegetables, tossing to coat. Grill the vegetables over medium-hot coals for 10 to 12 minutes or until of the desired degree of crispness, turning once.

YIELD: 6 SERVINGS

Nutrients Per Serving: **Cal 31; Prot 1 g; Carbo 7 g; T Fat <1 g; (Saturated Fat <1 g); Chol 0 mg; Fiber 2 g; Sod 169 mg**

Buy large quantities of red, orange, and yellow bell peppers when they are on sale. Wash, seed, and chop the bell peppers. Spread on a baking sheet sprayed lightly with vegetable oil. Freeze until firm. Transfer to freezer bags. The peppers will store for up to three months. This is not only economical, it is very convenient.

High Country Vegetable Bake

1	(14-ounce) can Italian-style tomatoes
1	cup ⅛-inch-thick carrot slices
1	(16-ounce) package frozen French-style green beans, thawed, drained
1	cup thinly sliced red bell pepper
1	cup sliced onion
2	cups sliced fresh mushrooms
1	tablespoon parsley flakes
½	teaspoon basil
¼	teaspoon garlic powder
⅛	teaspoon salt
⅛	teaspoon pepper
¼	cup grated Parmesan cheese

Drain the tomatoes, reserving 2 tablespoons of the juice; chop coarsely. Layer the carrots, green beans, red pepper, onion and mushrooms in the order listed in a 2-quart baking dish sprayed with nonstick cooking spray.

Sprinkle the parsley flakes, basil, garlic powder, salt and pepper over the prepared layers. Top with the tomatoes and drizzle with the reserved juice. Sprinkle with the cheese.

Bake, covered tightly, at 375 degrees for 1 hour. Sprinkle with additional parsley flakes if desired.

YIELD: 8 SERVINGS

Nutrients Per Serving: Cal 63; Prot 4 g; Carbo 10 g; T Fat 1 g; (Saturated Fat 1 g); Chol 2 mg; Fiber 3 g; Sod 194 mg

Barley and Pine Nuts

The chewy texture of roasted barley is wonderfully coupled with that of pine nuts. A nice departure from the usual rice pilaf.

1	tablespoon olive oil
1	cup pearl barley
1	small onion, chopped
1½	cups chicken broth
	salt and pepper to taste
⅓	cup pine nuts
¼	cup chopped fresh parsley

Heat the olive oil in a nonstick skillet. Add the barley and onion. Sauté until the barley is light brown and the onion is tender. Stir in the broth, salt and pepper.

Bring to a boil, stirring occasionally. Pour into a 2½-quart baking dish sprayed with nonstick cooking spray. Bake at 375 degrees for 45 minutes or until the liquid has been absorbed and the barley is tender.

Spread the pine nuts on a baking sheet. Toast at 375 degrees for 4 to 6 minutes or until light brown, stirring occasionally. Stir the pine nuts and parsley into the barley just before serving.

YIELD: 6 SERVINGS

Nutrients Per Serving: Cal 196; Prot 7 g; Carbo 29 g; T Fat 7 g;
(Saturated Fat 1 g); Chol 0 mg; Fiber 6 g; Sod 199 mg

Zucchini Couscous

A quick and delicious way to serve a new grain to your family.

1	medium zucchini, chopped
2	tablespoons chopped green onions
2	tablespoons reduced-sodium soy sauce
2	tablespoons white wine
1	garlic clove, minced
½	cup uncooked couscous
½	cup water
1½	teaspoons margarine

Combine the zucchini, green onions, soy sauce, white wine and garlic in a 2-quart microwave-safe dish and mix well. Microwave, covered, on Medium for 2 minutes. Stir in the couscous, water and margarine.

Microwave, covered, on High for 3 minutes. Let stand, covered, for 5 minutes before serving.

YIELD: 4 SERVINGS

Nutrients Per Serving: **Cal 115; Prot 4 g; Carbo 20 g; T Fat 2 g; (Saturated Fat <1 g); Chol 0 mg; Fiber 2 g; Sod 274 mg**

To boost your fiber intake dig into a variety of grains such as couscous, bulgur, or quinoa.

Savory Polenta

Unlike with the stove-top method, polenta prepared in the microwave does not require constant stirring.

3½ cups water
1   cup medium-grind cornmeal
½   teaspoon salt
1   teaspoon olive oil
1   small onion, minced
2   garlic cloves, minced
1½ teaspoons thyme
¼   teaspoon pepper
¼   cup grated Parmesan cheese

Combine the water, cornmeal and salt in a 2-quart microwave-safe dish. Microwave, covered, on High for 6 minutes; stir.

Heat the olive oil in a medium nonstick skillet. Add the onion, garlic and thyme and mix well. Sauté until the onion is tender.

Stir the onion mixture, pepper and cheese into the polenta.

Microwave, covered, on High for 5 to 6 minutes longer or until the polenta is creamy and tender. Serve immediately.

YIELD: 6 SERVINGS

Nutrients Per Serving: **Cal 106; Prot 4 g; Carbo 17 g; T Fat 3 g; (Saturated Fat 1 g); Chol 3 mg; Fiber 2 g; Sod 279 mg**

Keep healthful foods on hand. Store whole grain cereals, crackers, rice, and canned items such as beans, corn, and tuna in your pantry. Store reduced-fat cheeses, skim milk, fat-free yogurt, fruits, vegetables, tofu, lean beef, poultry, and/or fish in your refrigerator. Store prebaked pizza crusts, fat-free whipped topping, and frozen leftovers of soups and casseroles in your freezer.

Cinnamon Brown Rice

A delicious accompaniment to Oriental Fruited Pork on page 88.

2	cups water
1	cup brown rice
¼	teaspoon salt
½	cup dried cherries, dried cranberries or currants
¼	cup slivered almonds, toasted
1½	teaspoons cinnamon

Combine the water, brown rice and salt in a saucepan. Cook, covered, for 40 to 45 minutes or until the liquid has been absorbed and the rice is tender. Stir in the cherries, almonds and cinnamon.

YIELD: 6 SERVINGS

Nutrients Per Serving: **Cal 188; Prot 4 g; Carbo 34 g; T Fat 4 g; (Saturated Fat <1 g); Chol 0 mg; Fiber 3 g; Sod 101 mg**

Confetti Rice

1⅓	cups long grain rice
1½	teaspoons Cajun seasoning
1	cup chopped onion
1	cup finely chopped carrot
1	cup finely chopped celery
¾	cup finely chopped red bell pepper
½	cup finely chopped green bell pepper
2	garlic cloves, minced
2	tablespoons chopped fresh parsley

Cook the rice using package directions, omitting the salt and margarine and adding the Cajun seasoning.

Spray a large nonstick skillet with nonstick cooking spray. Heat over medium-high heat until hot. Add the onion, carrot, celery, red pepper, green pepper and garlic to the prepared skillet. Sauté until the vegetables are tender. Stir the onion mixture and parsley into the rice.

YIELD: 8 SERVINGS

Nutrients Per Serving: **Cal 138; Prot 3 g; Carbo 31 g; T Fat <1 g; (Saturated Fat <1 g); Chol 0 mg; Fiber 2 g; Sod 111 mg**

*H*erbs and spices are fragile and do not last for more than two to three years. To refresh your pantry, try the following: Empty your glass herb and spice jars, clean well, but do not remove the labels. Purchase replacement spices and herbs at a bulk-food store, co-op, or health food store where you can purchase them by the ounce. Purchase only what you can use within six months.

La Junta Lentils and Rice

1	cup dried lentils
1	small onion, chopped
2	teaspoons olive oil
1	cup uncooked rice
1	garlic clove, minced
3	cups chicken broth
¼	teaspoon turmeric
⅛	teaspoon ground ginger
⅛	teaspoon cinnamon
⅛	teaspoon pepper

Sort and rinse the lentils. Sauté the onion in 1 teaspoon of the olive oil in a skillet until tender.

Heat the remaining 1 teaspoon olive oil in a large skillet. Add the lentils, rice and garlic. Sauté until golden brown. Stir in the sautéed onion, broth, turmeric, ginger, cinnamon and pepper.

Bring to a boil; reduce heat. Simmer, covered, for 20 to 30 minutes or until all the liquid has been absorbed.

YIELD: 4 SERVINGS

Nutrients Per Serving: **Cal 389; Prot 21 g; Carbo 67 g; T Fat 4 g; (Saturated Fat 1 g); Chol 0 mg; Fiber 16 g; Sod 590 mg**

Pecan Rice

$\frac{1}{3}$	cup chopped pecans
1	tablespoon olive oil
$1\frac{1}{2}$	cups long grain rice
$\frac{1}{3}$	cup chopped onion
$2\frac{1}{2}$	cups chicken broth
$\frac{1}{4}$	teaspoon salt
$\frac{1}{4}$	teaspoon pepper
$\frac{1}{4}$	teaspoon thyme
$\frac{1}{4}$	cup chopped fresh parsley

Spread the pecans in a round glass baking dish. Toast at 350 degrees for 5 minutes or until fragrant and light brown.

Heat the olive oil in a saucepan over medium heat. Add the rice and onion. Sauté for 2 minutes. Stir in the broth, salt, pepper and thyme.

Bring to a boil; reduce heat. Simmer, covered, for 20 to 25 minutes or until the rice is tender. Stir in the pecans and parsley.

YIELD: 4 SERVINGS

Nutrients Per Serving: Cal 380; Prot 9 g; Carbo 59 g; T Fat 11 g; (Saturated Fat 1 g); Chol 0 mg; Fiber 2 g; Sod 636 mg

Microwave Risotto

Traditional risotto is a very time-consuming dish to prepare, but this microwave version is quick and easy.

1	cup arborio rice
¼	cup minced onion
1	tablespoon olive oil
3	cups chicken broth
1	tablespoon grated Parmesan cheese

Combine the rice, onion and olive oil in an 8x8-inch microwave-safe dish and mix well. Microwave on High for 2 minutes. Stir in the broth.
Microwave on High for 20 minutes, stirring every 5 minutes. Stir in the cheese. Let stand for 5 minutes; stir.

Tip: Add seafood, herbs and/or chopped vegetables during the last 3 minutes of the cooking process for variety.

YIELD: 4 SERVINGS

Nutrients Per Serving: Cal 288; Prot 9 g; Carbo 49 g; T Fat 5 g; (Saturated Fat 1 g); Chol 1 mg; Fiber 1 g; Sod 612 mg

Arborio rice creates its own creamy sauce and makes an elegant replacement for other types of rice.

Fresh Tomato Pesto over Angel Hair Pasta

A delicate showcase for vine-ripened tomatoes.

2	tablespoons extra-virgin olive oil
2	tablespoons whole pine nuts
½	cup chopped fresh basil
4	garlic cloves, minced
2	cups chopped Roma tomatoes (about 10 tomatoes)
¼	cup freshly grated Parmesan cheese
	salt and pepper to taste
8	ounces angel hair pasta

Using package directions bring the required amount of water for the pasta to a boil in a saucepan. Heat the olive oil in a saucepan over medium heat. Add the pine nuts and mix well.

Cook for 3 minutes or until light brown, stirring frequently. Stir in the basil and garlic. Sauté for 2 minutes. Add the tomatoes and mix well. Cook for 5 minutes, stirring frequently. Stir in the cheese, salt and pepper.

Add the pasta to the boiling water. Cook for 2 to 3 minutes; drain. Arrange the pasta on a serving platter. Spoon the tomato pesto over the pasta. Garnish with additional grated Parmesan cheese. Serve immediately.

YIELD: 4 SERVINGS

Nutrients Per Serving: Cal 313; Prot 12 g; Carbo 41 g; T Fat 12 g; (Saturated Fat 3 g); Chol 5 mg; Fiber 3 g; Sod 324 mg

Pasta with Beer Cheese Sauce

2   medium carrots, diagonally sliced
1   small zucchini, chopped
1   cup fresh whole mushrooms, cut into quarters
1   cup skim milk
3   tablespoons flour
¼   cup light beer
¾   cup shredded reduced-fat sharp Cheddar cheese
     salt and pepper to taste
8   ounces spinach fettuccini, cooked, drained

Bring enough water to cover the carrots to a boil in a saucepan. Add the carrots. Cook, covered, for 6 minutes. Add the zucchini and mushrooms. Cook, covered, for 2 to 3 minutes or just until the zucchini and mushrooms are tender-crisp; drain.

Combine the skim milk and flour in a jar with a tight-fitting lid. Cover the jar and shake to mix. Pour into a saucepan. Cook over medium heat until thickened, stirring constantly. Add the beer and mix well. Cook until heated through, stirring frequently. Remove from heat.

Add the cheese to the sauce and stir until the cheese melts. Add the vegetables and mix gently. Season with salt and pepper. Spoon over the hot fettuccini on a serving platter. Substitute tricolor rotini or fusilli for the spinach fettuccini if desired.

YIELD: 4 SERVINGS

Nutrients Per Serving: Cal 288; Prot 16 g; Carbo 44 g; T Fat 5 g; (Saturated Fat 3 g); Chol 12 mg; Fiber 4 g; Sod 287 mg

Lemon Caper Orzo

This recipe would make a quick, light-flavored side dish for fish or poultry.

2	quarts water
1	cup orzo
½	teaspoon salt
¼	cup chopped fresh parsley
3	tablespoons fresh lemon juice
2	tablespoons capers, rinsed, drained
1	teaspoon olive oil
½	teaspoon freshly ground pepper

Bring the water to a boil in a large saucepan. Stir in the orzo and salt. Boil for 10 to 12 minutes or until tender; drain. Stir the parsley, lemon juice, capers, olive oil and pepper into the orzo. Serve immediately.

Tip: Although orzo is a type of pasta, many mistake it for rice because of the similarity in shape and size. Expect a softer texture than that of rice.

YIELD: 6 SERVINGS

Nutrients Per Serving: Cal 114; Prot 4 g; Carbo 22 g; T Fat 1 g; (Saturated Fat <1 g); Chol 0 mg; Fiber 1 g; Sod 282 mg

Anyone at any age can benefit from physical activity. Try for thirty minutes of accumulated physical activity each day.

Mushroom and Pine Nut Pasta Sauce

This is a great way to jazz up your favorite commercially prepared pasta sauce.

¼	cup pine nuts
1	tablespoon olive oil
2	garlic cloves, crushed
3	cups sliced mushrooms
½	cup chopped zucchini
¼	cup chopped onion
1	(26-ounce) jar reduced-fat pasta sauce
1½	tablespoons basil
2	teaspoons oregano

Heat a small nonstick skillet over medium heat. Add the pine nuts. Toast for 3 to 5 minutes or until golden brown, stirring frequently.

Heat a large nonstick skillet over medium-high heat. Add the olive oil and garlic. Sauté for 1 minute. Stir in the mushrooms, zucchini and onion. Sauté for 5 to 8 minutes or until of the desired degree of crispness. Add the pasta sauce and mix well.

Simmer over low heat for 20 minutes, stirring occasionally. Stir in the basil and oregano. Add the pine nuts to the sauce or sprinkle over the top. Serve over your favorite hot cooked pasta.

Tip: Dried herbs have a stronger taste because the flavor is more concentrated. A good rule of thumb for substitution is to use 1 tablespoon of chopped fresh herbs per teaspoon of dried herbs.

YIELD: 8 SERVINGS

Nutrients Per Serving: Cal 86; Prot 3 g; Carbo 11 g; T Fat 4 g; (Saturated Fat 1 g); Chol 0 mg; Fiber 2 g; Sod 287 mg

BREADS
AND PIZZA

BREADS AND PIZZA

Colorado Gold Corn Bread

1   cup cornmeal
1   cup flour
1½   teaspoons baking powder
¼   teaspoon baking soda
1   (14-ounce) can cream-style corn
½   cup low-fat buttermilk
1   egg
1   tablespoon sugar
½   cup shredded sharp Cheddar cheese
1   jalapeño chile, seeded, chopped

Combine the cornmeal, flour, baking powder and baking soda in a bowl and mix well. Combine the corn, buttermilk, egg and sugar in a bowl and mix well. Add the cornmeal mixture and stir for 1 minute. Fold in the cheese and chile.

Pour the batter into an 8x8-inch baking pan sprayed with nonstick cooking spray. Place the pan on the bottom oven rack. Bake at 425 degrees for 30 to 40 minutes or until a wooden pick inserted in the center comes out clean. Let stand for 10 minutes. Cut into 9 squares.

Tip: Two cups of self-rising cornmeal mix may be substituted for the cornmeal, flour, baking powder and baking soda mixture.

YIELD: 9 SERVINGS

Nutrients Per Serving: Cal 177; Prot 6 g; Carbo 32 g; T Fat 4 g; (Saturated Fat 2 g); Chol 31 mg; Fiber 2 g; Sod 307 mg

Buttermilk has been used in many of our recipes as a replacement for fat. Although the name says "butter," the fat content is about the same as that of low-fat milk.

Flatirons Flatbread

An easy accompaniment to lasagna or spaghetti. Leftovers make great sandwiches.

½   cup lukewarm water
1   envelope fast-rising yeast
1   teaspoon sugar
2   cups flour
2   teaspoons olive oil
½   teaspoon salt
1   teaspoon Italian seasoning

Combine the lukewarm water, yeast and sugar in a bowl and mix well. Let stand for 5 minutes or until foamy. Stir in 1 cup of the flour, 1 teaspoon of the olive oil and salt. Add the remaining 1 cup flour gradually, kneading constantly until a soft dough forms.

Shape the dough into a disk approximately ½ inch thick. Place on a baking sheet or in a 9-inch round baking dish. Let rise for 15 minutes. Brush the top and side of the dough with the remaining 1 teaspoon olive oil. Sprinkle with the Italian seasoning. Bake at 350 degrees for 15 to 20 minutes or until golden brown. Cut into 6 wedges.

YIELD: 6 SERVINGS

Nutrients Per Serving: **Cal 171; Prot 5 g; Carbo 33 g; T Fat 2 g; (Saturated Fat <1 g); Chol 0 mg; Fiber 1 g; Sod 195 mg**

Lemon Poppy Seed Bread

POPPY SEED BREAD

3	cups flour
2¼	cups sugar
1½	tablespoons poppy seeds
1½	teaspoons salt
1½	teaspoons baking powder
1½	cups skim milk
½	cup unsweetened applesauce
¼	cup canola oil
¼	cup water
3	eggs
1½	teaspoons vanilla extract
1½	teaspoons lemon extract

LEMON GLAZE

½	cup confectioners' sugar
3	tablespoons lemon juice
¼	teaspoon vanilla extract

For the bread, combine the flour, sugar, poppy seeds, salt and baking powder in a mixer bowl and mix well. Add the skim milk, applesauce, canola oil, water, eggs and flavorings. Beat at low speed until blended, scraping the bowl occasionally.

Spoon the batter into 2 greased 5x9-inch loaf pans. Bake at 350 degrees for 1 hour. Cool in the pans for 5 minutes.

For the glaze, combine the confectioners' sugar, lemon juice and vanilla in a bowl and mix well. Drizzle over the warm bread. Cool in the pans for 15 minutes longer. Remove to a wire rack to cool completely.

YIELD: 24 SERVINGS

Nutrients Per Serving: Cal 181; Prot 3 g; Carbo 35 g; T Fat 3 g;
(Saturated Fat <1 g); Chol 27 mg; Fiber 1 g; Sod 192 mg

Harvest Pumpkin Bread

1	cup all-purpose flour
1	cup whole wheat flour
2	teaspoons baking powder
1½	teaspoons cinnamon
½	teaspoon salt
¼	teaspoon baking soda
¼	teaspoon ground cloves
1	cup sugar
¼	cup butter, softened
¼	cup sweetened applesauce
2	eggs
1	cup canned pumpkin
¼	cup orange juice

Combine the all-purpose flour, whole wheat flour, baking powder, cinnamon, salt, baking soda and cloves in a bowl and mix well. Beat the sugar, butter and applesauce in a mixer bowl for 5 minutes or until creamy and light, scraping the bowl occasionally.

Add the eggs 1 at a time, beating well after each addition. Add the pumpkin and orange juice. Beat until smooth. Stir in the flour mixture until blended.

Spoon the batter into a lightly greased 5x9-inch loaf pan. Bake at 350 degrees for 60 to 65 minutes or until a wooden pick inserted in the center comes out clean. Cool in the pan for several minutes. Remove to a wire rack to cool completely.

YIELD: 12 SERVINGS

Nutrients Per Serving: **Cal 196; Prot 4 g; Carbo 35 g; T Fat 5 g; (Saturated Fat 3 g); Chol 46 mg; Fiber 2 g; Sod 257 mg**

For fresh pumpkin or winter squash to use throughout the winter, choose a pumpkin or squash that will fit comfortably in your microwave. Rinse, remove the top, and discard the seeds; replace the top. Arrange in a microwave-safe dish. Microwave for 15 minutes or until tender. Let stand until cool. Peel, purée, and freeze in recipe-size portions.

Applesauce Bran Muffins

APPLESAUCE MUFFINS

1½	cups flour
1½	teaspoons baking powder
1	teaspoon cinnamon
1½	cups 100% bran cereal
1½	cups unsweetened applesauce
½	cup packed brown sugar
¼	cup margarine, melted
1	egg, lightly beaten
½	cup raisins (optional)

APPLESAUCE GLAZE

½	cup confectioners' sugar
1	tablespoon unsweetened applesauce

For the muffins, combine the flour, baking powder and cinnamon in a bowl and mix well. Combine the cereal, applesauce, brown sugar, margarine and egg in a bowl and mix well. Let stand for 5 minutes. Stir in the flour mixture. Fold in the raisins.

Spoon the batter into 12 greased muffin cups. Bake at 400 degrees for 18 to 22 minutes or until a wooden pick inserted in the center comes out clean and the muffins are light brown. Remove the muffins to a wire rack.

For the glaze, combine the confectioners' sugar and applesauce in a bowl and mix well. Spoon over the warm muffins. Serve immediately.

YIELD: 12 MUFFINS

Nutrients Per Muffin: Cal 197; Prot 3 g; Carbo 36 g; T Fat 5 g; (Saturated Fat 1 g); Chol 18 mg; Fiber 3 g; Sod 172 mg

It is easy to get the recommended amount of fiber each day—twenty to thirty-five grams—by choosing fiber-rich foods such as whole grains, fruits, vegetables, and legumes. Try the Applesauce Bran Muffins for breakfast or as a snack. They will give your diet a big fiber boost. In order to prevent digestive problems, add more fiber to your diet gradually. And don't forget to drink plenty of water.

Banana Chocolate Chip Muffins

1	cup all-purpose flour
¾	cup whole wheat flour
⅓	cup packed brown sugar
1	teaspoon baking powder
½	teaspoon baking soda
1	cup mashed bananas (about 2 bananas)
½	cup plain fat-free yogurt
1	egg
1	egg white
2	tablespoons canola oil
½	cup miniature chocolate chips

Line 12 muffin cups with paper liners or spray with nonstick cooking spray. Combine the all-purpose flour, whole wheat flour, brown sugar, baking powder and baking soda in a bowl and mix well.

Combine the bananas, yogurt, egg, egg white and canola oil in a bowl and mix well. Add to the flour mixture, stirring just until moistened. Fold in the chocolate chips.

Fill the muffin cups ⅔ full. Bake at 375 degrees for 20 to 25 minutes or until a wooden pick inserted in the center comes out clean. Remove to a wire rack.

Tip: The use of miniature chocolate chips is a great way to include chocolate in your recipes. Because they are small, the chocolate chips disperse well in batters. For most recipes, you can cut the amount of chocolate chips by half and still enjoy that rich chocolate flavor.

YIELD: 12 MUFFINS

Nutrients Per Muffin: Cal 189; Prot 4 g; Carbo 31 g; T Fat 6 g; (Saturated Fat 2 g); Chol 18 mg; Fiber 2 g; Sod 112 mg

Cinnamon Corn Muffins

1	cup cornmeal
½	cup unbleached all-purpose flour
½	cup whole wheat flour
2	tablespoons sugar
2½	teaspoons baking powder
2	teaspoons cinnamon
½	teaspoon salt
1¼	cups skim milk
½	cup sweetened applesauce
1	egg
1	tablespoon vegetable oil
	cinnamon to taste

Spray 12 muffin cups with nonstick cooking spray or line with paper liners. Combine the cornmeal, all-purpose flour, whole wheat flour, sugar, baking powder, 2 teaspoons cinnamon and salt in a bowl and mix well.

Whisk the skim milk, applesauce, egg and oil in a bowl until mixed. Add to the cornmeal mixture, stirring just until moistened. Spoon ¼ cup of the batter into each muffin cup. Sprinkle lightly with cinnamon to taste. Bake at 400 degrees for 17 to 20 minutes or until a wooden pick inserted in the center comes out clean. Remove to a wire rack.

YIELD: 12 MUFFINS

Nutrients Per Muffin: Cal 115; Prot 3 g; Carbo 21 g; T Fat 2 g;
(Saturated Fat <1 g); Chol 18 mg; Fiber 2 g; Sod 224 mg

Cranberry Muffins

¾ cup all-purpose flour
¾ cup whole wheat flour
½ cup packed brown sugar
2 teaspoons baking powder
1 teaspoon cinnamon
½ teaspoon ginger
¼ teaspoon salt
½ cup skim milk
¼ cup vegetable oil
¼ cup unsweetened applesauce
½ cup dried cranberries
¼ cup chopped pecans

Spray 12 muffin cups with nonstick cooking spray. Combine the all-purpose flour, whole wheat flour, brown sugar, baking powder, cinnamon, ginger and salt in a bowl and mix well.

Combine the skim milk, oil and applesauce in a bowl and mix well. Add to the flour mixture, stirring just until moistened. Fold in the cranberries and pecans. Spoon the batter into the prepared muffin cups. Bake at 350 degrees for 20 minutes or until a wooden pick inserted in the center comes out clean and the muffins are light brown. Remove to a wire rack.

YIELD: 12 MUFFINS

Nutrients Per Muffin: Cal 167; Prot 2 g; Carbo 26 g; T Fat 7 g;
(Saturated Fat 1 g); Chol <1 mg; Fiber 2 g; Sod 139 mg

Pumpkin Walnut Muffins

¼	cup chopped walnuts
1½	cups flour
2	teaspoons baking powder
¼	teaspoon cinnamon
¼	teaspoon nutmeg
¼	teaspoon salt
¾	cup canned pumpkin
½	cup packed brown sugar
¼	cup skim milk
¼	cup unsweetened applesauce
2	tablespoons canola oil
1	egg
1	egg white
½	cup raisins

Spray 12 muffin cups with nonstick cooking spray. Spread the walnuts in a round baking dish. Toast at 400 degrees for 5 minutes or until light brown, stirring occasionally.

Sift the flour, baking powder, cinnamon, nutmeg and salt into a bowl and mix well. Combine the pumpkin, brown sugar, skim milk, applesauce, canola oil, egg and egg white in a bowl and mix well. Add the flour mixture, walnuts and raisins, stirring just until moistened.

Spoon the batter into the prepared muffins cups. Bake at 400 degrees for 18 to 20 minutes or until a wooden pick inserted in the center comes out clean. Remove to a wire rack.

Tip: These muffins are best served warm. Reheat any leftovers in the microwave.

YIELD: 12 MUFFINS

Nutrients Per Muffin: Cal 163; Prot 3 g; Carbo 28 g; T Fat 4 g; (Saturated Fat <1 g); Chol 18 mg; Fiber 1 g; Sod 148 mg

Toasting nuts brings out a richer flavor, allowing you to use a smaller quantity and thus cut the fat grams. Nuts go further in a recipe if you chop more finely to distribute the flavor. If added texture is your goal, try adding other crunchy textures such as crisp cereals or reduced-fat crackers along with the nuts.

Apricot Scones

3	cups unbleached flour
2½	teaspoons baking powder
¼	cup sugar
½	teaspoon baking soda
½	teaspoon salt
¼	cup butter
1¼	cups low-fat buttermilk
1	cup chopped dried apricots
1	tablespoon sugar

Combine the flour, baking powder, ¼ cup sugar, baking soda and salt in a bowl and mix well. Cut in the butter with a pastry blender or 2 knives until crumbly. Add the buttermilk and apricots, stirring until the mixture adheres and forms a ball.

Place the dough on a baking sheet sprayed with nonstick cooking spray. Pat into a ¾-inch-thick circle. Score the dough into 12 wedges with a sharp knife. Sprinkle with 1 tablespoon sugar.

Bake at 450 degrees for 25 minutes or until a wooden pick inserted in the center comes out clean. Cool slightly. Cut into 12 wedges.

YIELD: 12 SCONES

Nutrients Per Scone: Cal 206; Prot 5 g; Carbo 38 g; T Fat 4 g; (Saturated Fat 3 g); Chol 11 mg; Fiber 2 g; Sod 319 mg

Orange Cranberry Scones

1⅓	cups flour
⅔	cup rolled oats
¼	cup sugar
1	teaspoon baking powder
½	teaspoon baking soda
½	teaspoon salt
	grated zest of 1 orange
3	tablespoons butter or margarine
½	cup low-fat buttermilk
3	ounces dried cranberries
2	tablespoons orange juice

Combine the flour, oats, sugar, baking powder, baking soda, salt and zest in a bowl and mix well. Cut in the butter with a pastry blender or 2 knives until crumbly. Combine the buttermilk, cranberries and orange juice in a bowl and mix well. Stir into the flour mixture with a fork.

Knead the dough on a lightly floured surface 8 to 10 times. Divide the dough into 2 equal portions. Shape each portion into a ball. Pat each portion into a ½-inch-thick circle. Cut each circle into 6 wedges.

Arrange the wedges 1 inch apart on a baking sheet. Bake at 425 degrees for 12 to 15 minutes or until light brown.

YIELD: 12 SCONES

Nutrients Per Scone: Cal 139; Prot 3 g; Carbo 24 g; T Fat 3 g;
(Saturated Fat 2 g); Chol 8 mg; Fiber 2 g; Sod 231 mg

Frijol Pizza

1 (16-ounce) prebaked pizza crust
1 teaspoon olive oil
⅓ cup chopped red onion
2 garlic cloves, minced
½ (15-ounce) can black beans, drained, rinsed
½ (15-ounce) can garbanzo beans, drained, rinsed
½ (15-ounce) can red kidney beans, drained, rinsed
⅔ cup pizza sauce
⅓ cup chopped fresh cilantro
1 cup shredded Monterey Jack cheese

Arrange the pizza crust on an ungreased baking sheet. Heat the olive oil in a large nonstick skillet. Add the red onion.
Sauté for 3 minutes. Add the garlic. Sauté for 2 minutes longer. Stir in the beans and pizza sauce.
Cook for 3 minutes, stirring occasionally. Spread the bean mixture evenly over the pizza crust. Sprinkle with the cilantro. Top with the cheese. Bake at 450 degrees for 10 to 12 minutes or until light brown and bubbly.

YIELD: 4 SERVINGS

Nutrients Per Serving: **Cal 569; Prot 26 g; Carbo 84 g; T Fat 15 g; (Saturated Fat 7 g); Chol 25 mg; Fiber 10 g; Sod 1481 mg**

Southwest Beef and Chile Pizza

1	(16-ounce) prebaked pizza crust
8	ounces ground beef
1¼	cups chunky salsa
1	(4-ounce) can diced green chiles, drained
2	medium plum tomatoes, chopped
⅓	cup thinly sliced red onion
½	cup each shredded reduced-fat sharp Cheddar cheese and part-skim mozzarella cheese
2	tablespoons chopped fresh cilantro

Arrange the pizza crust on an ungreased baking sheet. Brown the ground beef in a large skillet over medium heat, stirring until crumbly; drain. Spread the salsa over the pizza crust. Layer with the ground beef, chiles, tomatoes and red onion. Sprinkle with the Cheddar cheese and mozzarella cheese. Bake at 450 degrees for 10 to 12 minutes or until the cheese melts. Sprinkle with the cilantro. Cut into wedges.

YIELD: 4 SERVINGS

Nutrients Per Serving: Cal 523; Prot 30 g; Carbo 64 g; T Fat 17 g; (Saturated Fat 7 g); Chol 56 mg; Fiber 3 g; Sod 1706 mg

Barbecue Chicken Pizza

1	whole boneless skinless chicken breast, cut into ½-inch cubes
1	teaspoon olive oil
⅔	cup favorite barbecue sauce
1	(16-ounce) prebaked pizza crust
⅓	cup chopped green onions
1	cup shredded part-skim mozzarella cheese

Sauté the chicken in the olive oil in a nonstick skillet over medium heat for 5 minutes or until cooked through. Add 2 tablespoons of the barbecue sauce and stir until coated. Spread remaining barbecue sauce over pizza crust. Top with the chicken mixture and green onions. Sprinkle with the cheese. Bake at 450 degrees for 10 minutes or until cheese melts.

YIELD: 4 SERVINGS

Nutrients Per Serving: Cal 540; Prot 44 g; Carbo 60 g; T Fat 13 g; (Saturated Fat 5 g); Chol 89 mg; Fiber 2 g; Sod 1166

There is something wonderful about the taste of pizza, but a quick comparison of commercial pizza with ours will convince you to do the toppings yourself. Getting creative with the sauce, limiting the cheese, and selecting reduced-fat toppings can add a healthy pizzazz to your pizza. Try some of these pizza ideas:

*

Grilled Garlic Herb Pizza Crust (page 182) with pesto, mozzarella cheese, and Fire-Grilled Vegetables (page 151). →

Veggie Pita Pizzas

¼	cup pine nuts
1	tablespoon olive oil
2	tablespoons basil or oregano
4	cups torn fresh spinach
2	large whole wheat pita pockets, split
1	(14-ounce) can diced tomatoes, drained
¼	cup sliced drained black olives
	salt and pepper to taste
1	cup shredded part-skim mozzarella cheese

 Spread the pine nuts in a 3-quart saucepan. Toast over medium heat for 5 minutes or until light brown, stirring often. Cool slightly. Stir in the olive oil and basil. Cool for several minutes. Add the spinach, stirring until coated. Transfer to a bowl.

Arrange the pita halves on a baking sheet lined with foil. Spread ¼ of the spinach mixture on each pita half. Combine the tomatoes and black olives in the empty 3-quart saucepan, stirring to mix with the olive oil and basil remaining in the saucepan. Season with salt and pepper. Spoon ¼ of the tomato mixture onto each pita half and spread evenly over the spinach mixture.

Sprinkle each pita with ¼ cup of the cheese. Broil for 2 to 3 minutes or until the cheese melts and is light brown.

Tip: Purchase commercially packaged spinach to make preparation of this recipe even quicker.

YIELD: 4 SERVINGS

Nutrients Per Serving: Cal 293; Prot 15 g; Carbo 30 g; T Fat 14 g; (Saturated Fat 4 g); Chol 16 mg; Fiber 5 g; Sod 611 mg

Crusty Whole Wheat Pizza Crust

1½   teaspoons dry yeast
1½   cups whole wheat flour
1½   cups all-purpose flour
½   teaspoon salt
2   teaspoons olive oil
1   cup water

Place the yeast, whole wheat flour, all-purpose flour, salt, olive oil and water in the order listed in a bread machine. Set the machine on the manual cycle and let the dough be mixed and rise. Remove the dough at end of cycle and place the dough on a 14- or 16-inch pizza pan sprayed with nonstick cooking spray.

Pat the dough over the bottom and up the side of the pizza pan. Roll back approximately ½ inch of the dough around the edge to form a thicker edge if desired. Prick generously with a fork. Bake at 450 degrees for 10 to 15 minutes or until light brown. Top with you favorite sauce, toppings and cheese.

YIELD: 1 (14- OR 16-INCH) PIZZA CRUST

Nutrients Per Pizza Crust: **Cal 1390; Prot 46 g; Carbo 276 g; T Fat 14 g; (Saturated Fat 2 g); Chol 0 mg; Fiber 28 g; Sod 1178 mg**

*
Crusty Whole Wheat Pizza Crust with barbecue sauce, Cheddar and mozzarella cheese, Canadian bacon, water-pack artichoke hearts, and sliced tomatoes.
*
Grilled Garlic Herb Pizza Crust (page 182) brushed with olive oil, sprinkled with minced garlic, and topped with Caponata (page 19).

d Garlic Herb Pizza Crust

	oon olive oil
	oon minced garlic
1	tablespoon minced fresh basil
1	teaspoon pepper
1½	teaspoons dry yeast
1	teaspoon sugar
1¼	cups lukewarm water
¼	cup cornmeal
1	teaspoon salt
3	cups bread flour
2	teaspoons olive oil
½	teaspoon salt

Heat 1 tablespoon olive oil in a skillet. Add the garlic, basil and pepper. Cook over low heat for 3 minutes or until the garlic is tender. Let stand until cool.

Sprinkle the yeast and sugar over ¼ cup of the lukewarm water in a bowl. Let stand until the yeast begins to swell. Combine the garlic mixture, remaining 1 cup lukewarm water, cornmeal and 1 teaspoon salt in a bowl and mix well. Stir in the yeast mixture. Add the bread flour 1 cup at a time, mixing until a soft dough forms. Knead the dough on a lightly floured surface until smooth and elastic, adding additional flour as needed to prevent the dough from sticking.

Place the dough in a bowl sprayed with nonstick cooking spray, turning to coat the surface. Let rise, covered with a damp tea towel, for 2 hours or until doubled in bulk. Divide the dough into 2 equal portions. Roll each portion into a 14-inch circle on a lightly floured surface, sprinkling with additional flour as needed.

Brush the top of each circle with the olive oil and sprinkle with ½ teaspoon salt. Grill oil side down over hot coals for 2 to 3 minutes or until dark brown grill marks appear; turn. Grill until light brown. Arrange the pizza crusts on a baking sheet. Sprinkle with your favorite toppings. Broil for 1 to 2 minutes or until brown and bubbly.

Tip: To prepare in a bread machine, combine the garlic mixture, lukewarm water, cornmeal, 1 teaspoon salt, sugar and bread flour in the bread machine pan in the order recommended by the manufacturer. Set the machine on the dough cycle. Add the yeast to the dispenser. Remove the dough from the bread machine at the end of the cycle and proceed as directed above.

YIELD: 8 SERVINGS

Nutrients Per Serving: Cal 232; Prot 7 g; Carbo 42 g; T Fat 4 g; (Saturated Fat 1 g); Chol 0 mg; Fiber 2 g; Sod 439 mg

DESSERTS

DESSERTS

Cappuccino Cheesecake

½   cup chocolate wafer crumbs
3   tablespoons instant espresso powder
3   tablespoons coffee liqueur
1½ cups fat-free or 1% cottage cheese
8   ounces fat-free cream cheese, softened
8   ounces tub-style reduced-fat cream cheese
1   cup sugar
2   tablespoons flour
6   egg whites
¼   teaspoon cinnamon
¼   teaspoon salt

Reserve 1 teaspoon of the crumbs. Sprinkle the remaining crumbs over the bottom of a 9-inch springform pan sprayed with nonstick cooking spray. Combine the espresso powder and liqueur in a bowl, stirring until the powder dissolves.

Process the cottage cheese in a blender until smooth. Add the cream cheese, sugar, flour, egg whites, cinnamon, salt and espresso mixture. Process until blended. Spoon into the prepared pan.

Bake at 325 degrees for 65 to 70 minutes or until the cheesecake puffs and the center is almost set. Sprinkle with the reserved crumbs. Cool in pan on a wire rack. Chill, covered, for 4 to 10 hours. Remove side of pan and slice.

YIELD: 12 SERVINGS

Nutrients Per Serving: **Cal 198; Prot 11 g; Carbo 28 g; T Fat 4 g; (Saturated Fat 2 g); Chol 13 mg; Fiber <1 g; Sod 399 mg**

Fat-free cream cheese can be a tricky ingredient to use. It will create small curds when blended unless it is first softened to room temperature and blended with reduced-fat cream cheese.

Caramel Bananas

4   large ripe bananas
⅓   cup packed brown sugar
1   tablespoon margarine, melted
1½   teaspoons lemon juice
¼   teaspoon cinnamon
1½   cups frozen vanilla yogurt

Cut the bananas lengthwise into halves. Arrange the banana halves cut side up on a baking sheet sprayed with nonstick cooking spray. Bake at 450 degrees for 4 minutes.
   Combine the brown sugar, margarine, lemon juice and cinnamon in a bowl and mix well. Drizzle over the bananas. Bake for 3 minutes longer. Cut each banana half crosswise into 3 equal portions. Arrange over the yogurt in dessert bowls. Drizzle with any extra sauce.

YIELD: 4 SERVINGS

Nutrients Per Serving: **Cal 358; Prot 8 g; Carbo 72 g; T Fat 7 g; (Saturated Fat 2 g); Chol 38 mg; Fiber 4 g; Sod 79 mg**

Gingered Peaches

A delightful way to use our Western Slope produce.

4	ripe peaches
1	(12-ounce) can peach nectar
1	tablespoon white vinegar
1	(6-inch) cinnamon stick
½	teaspoon whole cloves
4	(quarter-size) slices peeled fresh gingerroot
4	ounces tub-style reduced-fat cream cheese
1½	tablespoons sugar
2	tablespoons minced candied ginger
1	or 2 gingersnap cookies, crushed

Bring enough water to cover the peaches to a boil in a saucepan. Add the peaches. Remove from heat. Let stand for 1 minute; drain. Transfer the peaches to a bowl of cold water. Let stand until cool; drain. Peel the peaches, cut into halves and discard the pits.

Combine the peach nectar, vinegar, cinnamon stick, cloves and gingerroot in a saucepan. Simmer for 5 minutes, stirring occasionally. Add the peach halves. Simmer for 15 minutes or until the peaches are tender but firm, stirring occasionally. Remove the peaches to a bowl with a slotted spoon, reserving the liquid. Strain the reserved liquid, discarding the solid ingredients. Chill the peaches and liquid to room temperature.

Beat 3 tablespoons of the reserved liquid, cream cheese and sugar in a mixer bowl until creamy. Fold in the candied ginger. Drizzle equal amounts of the remaining reserved liquid over the bottom of 4 dessert plates. Place the peach halves on the prepared plates. Spoon 1 tablespoon of the cream cheese mixture into the center of each peach half. Sprinkle with the gingersnap crumbs. Serve immediately.

Tip: May substitute one drained 29-ounce can water-pack peach halves for the fresh peaches, omitting the peeling process.

YIELD: 4 SERVINGS

Nutrients Per Serving: Cal 209; Prot 4 g; Carbo 39 g; T Fat 5 g; (Saturated Fat 3 g); Chol 13 mg; Fiber 3 g; Sod 162 mg

Poached Pears in Spiced Red Wine Sauce

This elegant dessert makes a wonderful dish to serve when company comes.

1½	cups dry red wine
1	cup water
½	cup packed dark brown sugar
3	tablespoons honey
1	tablespoon fresh lemon juice
1	teaspoon vanilla extract
1	(3-inch) cinnamon stick, broken into halves
10	black peppercorns
8	whole cloves
4	firm ripe Bartlett or Bosc pears
2	tablespoons cornstarch

Combine the red wine, water, brown sugar, honey, lemon juice, vanilla, cinnamon stick, peppercorns and cloves in a 3-quart microwave-safe dish and mix well. Microwave on High for 5 minutes or until the poaching mixture comes to a boil.

Peel and core the pears, leaving the stems intact. Arrange the pears stem side up in the poaching mixture. Microwave, covered, on High for 10 minutes or until the pears are tender. Cool for 5 minutes. Remove the pears with a slotted spoon to a platter.

Strain the poaching liquid, discarding the cinnamon stick, cloves and peppercorns. Pour half the liquid into a microwave-safe dish, discarding the remainder of the liquid. Mix the cornstarch with enough water in a bowl until of the consistency of a thin paste. Whisk the cornstarch mixture into the poaching liquid until blended. Microwave on Medium for 5 minutes or until the sauce thickens and loses its cloudy appearance, stirring at 1-minute intervals.

Spoon 2 tablespoons of the sauce into each of 4 dessert bowls. Arrange 1 pear in each bowl. Drizzle the remaining sauce evenly over the pears.

Tip: To core a pear, hold the pear in one hand. Using a small paring knife, cut a round hole approximately ½ inch in diameter up through the bottom of the pear, stopping approximately ¾ of the way up the pear. Discard the core. An apple corer may be used to remove the core. Cut about ¼ inch off the base of the pear to allow the pear to sit flat.

YIELD: 4 SERVINGS

Nutrients Per Serving: Cal 330; Prot 1 g; Carbo 70 g; T Fat 1 g; (Saturated Fat <1 g); Chol 0 mg; Fiber 4 g; Sod 16 mg

Cranapple Crisp

OAT TOPPING

⅔   cup quick-cooking oats

¼   cup packed brown sugar

3   tablespoons whole wheat flour

3   tablespoons thawed frozen unsweetened apple juice concentrate

½   teaspoon cinnamon

CRANAPPLE FILLING

8   cups thinly sliced peeled apples (about 5 apples)

½   cup chopped cranberries

⅓   cup packed brown sugar

1   tablespoon cornstarch

1   tablespoon thawed frozen unsweetened apple juice concentrate

1   cup fat-free whipped topping

For the topping, combine the oats, brown sugar, whole wheat flour, apple juice concentrate and cinnamon in a bowl and mix well.

For the filling, toss the apples, cranberries, brown sugar, cornstarch and apple juice concentrate in a bowl until mixed. Spread the apple mixture in a 2½-quart baking dish sprayed with nonstick cooking spray. Sprinkle with the oat topping.

Bake at 375 degrees for 30 minutes. Cover loosely with foil. Bake for 15 minutes longer or until bubbly and golden brown. Serve warm topped with the whipped topping.

Tip: If cranberries are not available, just use apples and decrease the brown sugar for the filling to ¼ cup.

YIELD: 6 SERVINGS

Nutrients Per Serving: Cal 268; Prot 3 g; Carbo 64 g; T Fat 1 g;
(Saturated Fat <1 g); Chol 0 mg; Fiber 5 g; Sod 19 mg

Fanciful Pudding

An elegant, yet light dessert.

1	(4-ounce) package vanilla instant pudding mix
2	cups skim milk
½	cup fat-free whipped topping
1	cup fresh raspberries
1	cup fresh blueberries
1	cup sliced fresh strawberries
4	whole fresh strawberries (optional)

 Prepare the pudding mix using package directions, substituting 2 cups skim milk for the milk. Fold in the whipped topping.

Spoon 2 tablespoons of the pudding and ¼ cup of the raspberries into each of 4 wine or parfait glasses. Alternate layers of the remaining pudding with the blueberries and sliced strawberries, ending with the pudding. Chill, covered, until serving time. Top with whole strawberries sliced into a fan shape.

YIELD: 4 SERVINGS

Nutrients Per Serving: **Cal 197; Prot 5 g; Carbo 44 g; T Fat 1 g; (Saturated Fat <1 g); Chol 2 mg; Fiber 4 g; Sod 427 mg**

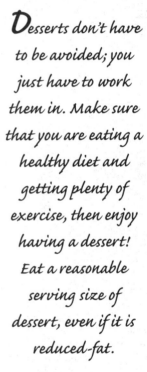

Desserts don't have to be avoided; you just have to work them in. Make sure that you are eating a healthy diet and getting plenty of exercise, then enjoy having a dessert! Eat a reasonable serving size of dessert, even if it is reduced-fat.

Speedy Rice Pudding

2½   cups skim milk
¼   teaspoon salt
1   cup instant rice
⅓   cup sugar
2   tablespoons cornstarch
¼   teaspoon cinnamon
3   tablespoons water
1   egg, beaten
½   teaspoon vanilla extract
¼   cup raisins
      nutmeg to taste

Combine the skim milk and salt in a saucepan. Cook over medium-high heat until the mixture comes to a boil, stirring constantly. Stir in the rice. Remove from heat. Let stand, covered, for 5 minutes.

Combine the sugar, cornstarch and cinnamon in a bowl and mix well. Stir in the water, egg and vanilla. Add a small amount of the hot rice mixture and mix well. Stir the egg mixture into the rice mixture. Add the raisins and mix well.

Cook over medium heat for 10 minutes or until thickened, stirring constantly. Spoon into 4 custard cups. Sprinkle with nutmeg. Let stand for 10 minutes. Serve warm.

YIELD: 4 SERVINGS

Nutrients Per Serving: Cal 269; Prot 9 g; Carbo 55 g; T Fat 2 g;
(Saturated Fat 1 g); Chol 56 mg; Fiber 1 g; Sod 243 mg

Light Tiramisù

Traditional Tiramisù is made with cream and other high-fat ingredients. While our recipe is certainly not low in fat and calories, it beats the 35 grams of fat and 440 calories found in traditional versions.

8	ounces mascarpone cheese, softened
4	ounces fat-free cream cheese, softened
½	cup confectioners' sugar
1	cup frozen fat-free whipped topping, thawed
⅔	cup hot water
2	teaspoons instant coffee granules
¼	cup brandy or coffee liqueur
2	(3-ounce) packages ladyfingers
1½	teaspoons baking cocoa

Combine the mascarpone cheese, cream cheese and confectioners' sugar in a mixer bowl. Beat until smooth, scraping the bowl occasionally. Fold in the whipped topping.

Bring the hot water to a boil in a saucepan. Add the coffee granules, stirring until the granules dissolve. Let stand until cool. Stir in the brandy.

Arrange 1 package of the ladyfingers over the bottom and up the side of a 2-quart soufflé dish. Drizzle or brush with half the coffee mixture. Spread with half the mascarpone cheese mixture. Repeat the layering process with the remaining ladyfingers, remaining coffee mixture and remaining mascarpone cheese mixture. Sift the baking cocoa over the top. Chill, covered, for 8 to 10 hours.

YIELD: 10 SERVINGS

Nutrients Per Serving: Cal 223; Prot 5 g; Carbo 20 g; T Fat 12 g; (Saturated Fat 6 g); Chol 92 mg; Fiber <1 g; Sod 97 mg

Fresh Strawberry Torte

An easy, but oh so elegant, dessert.

3	egg whites
¾	cup sugar
1	teaspoon vanilla extract
¾	cup finely crushed soda crackers
½	cup chopped pecans
1	pound strawberries, sliced
1	tablespoon Grand Marnier or other orange liqueur
8	ounces frozen fat-free whipped topping, thawed

Beat the egg whites in a mixer bowl until soft peaks form. Add the sugar gradually, beating constantly. Add the vanilla. Beat until stiff peaks form. Fold in the cracker crumbs and pecans. Spread over the bottom and up the side of a 9-inch pie plate sprayed with nonstick cooking spray. Bake at 325 degrees for 30 minutes or until light brown. Let stand until cool.

Mound the strawberries in the meringue crust. Drizzle with the Grand Marnier. Spread with the whipped topping. Chill, covered, for 2 to 10 hours. Garnish with additional strawberries.

Tip: This recipe can easily be doubled for large crowds. Spread the meringue in a circle on a greased baking sheet instead of spreading in a pie plate if desired.

YIELD: 8 SERVINGS

Nutrients Per Serving: Cal 231; Prot 3 g; Carbo 39 g; T Fat 6 g; (Saturated Fat 1 g); Chol 0 mg; Fiber 2 g; Sod 140 mg

Small amounts of liqueurs or wine can be used sparingly to add sophistication, moisture, and flavor to desserts.

All of the recipes in simply Colorado, Too! have been developed and tested at high altitude. Our thinner blanket of air in high altitudes causes water to boil at a lower temperature, rapid evaporation of moisture, and leavening agents to rise more rapidly. If you take these recipes to sea level and feel that adjustments would improve the results, try one or more of the following:
*
Expect rice and pasta to cook faster at sea level. →

Applesauce Spice Cake

1	cup all-purpose flour
1	cup whole wheat flour
2½	teaspoons cinnamon
2	teaspoons baking soda
¾	teaspoon nutmeg
¾	teaspoon ground cloves
6	egg whites
1¼	cups sugar
1½	cups chunky unsweetened applesauce
⅓	cup low-fat buttermilk
1	teaspoon vanilla extract
1	cup raisins
1	recipe Fluffy Cream Cheese Frosting (page 195)

Combine the all-purpose flour, whole wheat flour, cinnamon, baking soda, nutmeg and cloves in a bowl and mix well. Beat the egg whites in a mixer bowl until soft peaks form. Add the sugar gradually, beating constantly until stiff peaks form. Stir in the applesauce, buttermilk and vanilla.

Add the flour mixture to the batter, stirring just until combined. Fold in the raisins. Spoon into a 9x13-inch cake pan sprayed with nonstick cooking spray. Bake at 350 degrees for 35 to 40 minutes or until a wooden pick inserted in the center comes out clean. Cool in pan on a wire rack. Spread with the Fluffy Cream Cheese Frosting.

YIELD: 15 SERVINGS

Nutrients Per Serving: Cal 248; Prot 5 g; Carbo 52 g; T Fat 3 g; (Saturated Fat 2 g); Chol 7 mg; Fiber 2 g; Sod 280 mg
Nutritional information includes the frosting.

Fluffy Cream Cheese Frosting

The great taste of cream cheese frosting with a fraction of the fat.

8   ounces tub-style reduced-fat cream cheese
1   (7-ounce) jar marshmallow creme
1   teaspoon vanilla extract

 Stir the cream cheese in a bowl until creamy. Add the marshmallow creme and vanilla and mix just until blended. Overmixing will cause the frosting to become runny.

Tip: Compare our Fluffy Cream Cheese Frosting to the traditional versions that add 100 calories and 5 grams of fat to every serving of cake.

YIELD: 15 SERVINGS

Nutrients Per Serving: **Cal 77; Prot 1 g; Carbo 12 g; T Fat 2 g; (Saturated Fat 2 g); Chol 7 mg; Fiber 0 g; Sod 82 mg**

*
For baked goods, increase the leavening (baking powder, baking soda, cream of tartar) by $\frac{1}{2}$ to $\frac{2}{3}$ teaspoon for each teaspoon called for in the recipe.
*
In baked goods and sauces, decrease 1 to 2 tablespoons of the liquid for each cup of liquid called for in the recipe.
*
Lower skillet/wok and baking temperatures by 25 degrees.

Triple-Chocolate Bundt Cake

Intense chocolate flavor!

2	tablespoons baking cocoa
1	(2-layer) package devil's food cake mix
1	(4-ounce) package chocolate fudge instant pudding mix
1	cup plain fat-free yogurt
1	(2-ounce) jar baby food prunes
½	cup water
2	eggs
2	egg whites
¼	cup reduced-fat mayonnaise
1	teaspoon vanilla extract
½	cup chocolate chips
	confectioners' sugar to taste

Spray a 12-cup bundt pan with nonstick cooking spray. Dust with the baking cocoa. Combine the cake mix, pudding mix, yogurt, prunes, water, eggs, egg whites, mayonnaise and vanilla in a mixer bowl. Beat until blended, scraping the bowl occasionally. Stir in the chocolate chips.

Spoon the batter into the prepared pan. Bake at 350 degrees for 50 minutes or until a wooden pick inserted in the center comes out clean. Cool in pan for 20 minutes. Remove to a wire rack to cool completely. Dust with confectioners' sugar just before serving.

YIELD: 16 SERVINGS

Nutrients Per Serving: Cal 222; Prot 5 g; Carbo 35 g; T Fat 8 g;
(Saturated Fat 3 g); Chol 34 mg; Fiber 1 g; Sod 370 mg

Chocolate Yogurt Cake

2	cups flour
1½	cups sugar
½	cup baking cocoa
2	teaspoons baking soda
½	teaspoon salt
4	egg whites, lightly beaten
¼	cup vegetable oil
2	(2-ounce) jars baby food prunes
⅓	cup chocolate syrup
1	cup plain fat-free yogurt
1	egg
1½	teaspoons vanilla extract
	confectioners' sugar to taste

Combine the flour, sugar, baking cocoa, baking soda and salt in a mixer bowl and mix well. Combine the egg whites, oil, prunes and chocolate syrup in a bowl and mix well. Stir in the yogurt, egg and vanilla.

Add the egg mixture to the flour mixture. Beat at low speed until blended, scraping the bowl constantly. Beat at medium speed for 2 minutes, scraping the bowl frequently.

Spoon the batter into a lightly oiled 9x13-inch cake pan. Bake at 350 degrees for 25 to 35 minutes or until a wooden pick inserted in the center comes out clean. Cool in pan on a wire rack. Sprinkle with confectioners' sugar.

YIELD: 15 SERVINGS

Nutrients Per Serving: Cal 218; Prot 4 g; Carbo 41 g; T Fat 5 g; (Saturated Fat 1 g); Chol 15 mg; Fiber 2 g; Sod 277 mg

Many chocolate desserts use baking chocolate, which is high in fat as an ingredient. As a healthy substitution, replace every ounce of baking chocolate with 3 tablespoons baking cocoa and 1 tablespoon prune purée.

Banana Strawberry Frozen Yogurt

2   ripe bananas
1   cup sliced strawberries
1   cup plain fat-free yogurt
½   cup sifted confectioners' sugar
1   teaspoon vanilla extract

Chill a mixer bowl and beaters. Combine the bananas, strawberries, yogurt, confectioners' sugar and vanilla in a food processor container. Process until smooth. Spoon into a 9x9-inch dish. Freeze, covered, for 2 to 3 hours or until firm.

Break the frozen mixture into small pieces and transfer to the chilled mixer bowl. Beat until smooth but not liquid. Return the banana mixture to the 9x9-inch dish. Freeze, covered, for 1 hour or until firm. Spoon into dessert bowls. May freeze in a 4-quart ice cream freezer using manufacturer's directions.

Tip: This recipe can also be used to make a refreshing slush. Spoon the banana mixture into ice cube trays and freeze until firm. Process the frozen mixture in a blender or food processor until smooth. Pour into 8 chilled glasses. Serve immediately.

YIELD: 4 SERVINGS

Nutrients Per Serving: Cal 140; Prot 3 g; Carbo 34 g; T Fat <1 g; (Saturated Fat <1 g); Chol 1 mg; Fiber 2 g; Sod 35 mg

Almond Spice Biscotti

¾ cup packed brown sugar

1 egg

2 egg whites

2 tablespoons canola oil

1 teaspoon vanilla extract

¾ teaspoon almond extract

3 cups flour

½ cup chopped almonds

1 teaspoon cinnamon

¾ teaspoon baking soda

¾ teaspoon salt

½ teaspoon ground cloves

½ teaspoon orange zest

¼ cup orange juice

Combine the brown sugar, egg, egg whites, canola oil and flavorings in a bowl and mix well. Combine the flour, almonds, cinnamon, baking soda, salt, cloves and orange zest in a bowl and mix well. Add the flour mixture to the egg mixture and mix well. Add the orange juice, stirring until a stiff dough forms.

Shape the dough into a 16-inch log on a lightly floured surface, kneading as necessary. Transfer the log to a cookie sheet sprayed with nonstick cooking spray. Pat 1 inch thick. Bake at 350 degrees for 30 minutes or until light brown and cracked on top. Cool for 10 minutes.

Reduce the oven temperature to 325 degrees. Transfer the log to a hard surface. Cut the log diagonally with a serrated knife into ¼- to ⅓-inch slices. Arrange the slices in a single layer on 2 ungreased cookie sheets. Bake for 10 minutes; turn. Bake for 10 minutes longer. Transfer to a wire rack to cool. Store in an airtight container for up to 1 month.

YIELD: 40 BISCOTTI

Nutrients Per Biscotti: **Cal 69; Prot 2 g; Carbo 12 g; T Fat 2 g; (Saturated Fat <1 g); Chol 5 mg; Fiber <1 g; Sod 74 mg**

Brownie Oat Chews

1	cup quick-cooking oats
⅔	cup flour
⅔	cup sugar
⅓	cup baking cocoa
1	teaspoon baking powder
¼	teaspoon salt
2	egg whites
⅓	cup light corn syrup
1	teaspoon vanilla extract

 Combine the oats, flour, sugar, baking cocoa, baking powder and salt in a bowl and mix well. Add the egg whites, corn syrup and vanilla, stirring just until moistened; dough will be very thick.

Drop by rounded teaspoonfuls onto a cookie sheet sprayed with nonstick cooking spray. Bake at 350 degrees for 10 minutes. Cool on cookie sheet for 5 minutes. Remove to wire rack to cool completely.

YIELD: 24 COOKIES

Nutrients Per Cookie: Cal 68; Prot 2 g; Carbo 15 g; T Fat <1 g; (Saturated Fat <1 g); Chol 0 mg; Fiber 1 g; Sod 55 mg

Don't ever reveal that the dessert you just made is reduced-fat. Make it your little secret.

Outrageous Orange Cookies

COOKIES

1	cup unbleached all-purpose flour
1/3	cup whole wheat flour
1/2	teaspoon baking powder
1/2	teaspoon salt
1/4	teaspoon baking soda
1/2	cup sugar
3	tablespoons shortening
3	tablespoons butter, softened
1	egg
1/3	cup low-fat buttermilk
2	tablespoons orange juice
2	teaspoons finely shredded orange zest

ORANGE FROSTING

1½	cups sifted confectioners' sugar
1½	teaspoons finely shredded orange zest
1½	tablespoons orange juice

For the cookies, combine the all-purpose flour, whole wheat flour, baking powder, salt and baking soda in a bowl and mix well. Beat the sugar, shortening and butter in a mixer bowl until creamy, scraping the bowl frequently. Add the egg and beat until light and fluffy. Beat in the buttermilk, orange juice and zest. Add the dry ingredients, stirring just until moistened.

Drop the dough by mounded teaspoonfuls onto an ungreased cookie sheet. Bake at 350 degrees for 10 minutes; do not brown. Remove to a wire rack to cool completely.

For the frosting, combine the confectioners' sugar and zest in a bowl. Add enough of the orange juice to make of a spreadable consistency. Spread over the cooled cookies.

YIELD: 30 COOKIES

Nutrients Per Cookie: Cal 78; Prot 1 g; Carbo 13 g; T Fat 3 g; (Saturated Fat 1 g); Chol 10 mg; Fiber <1 g; Sod 74 mg

Citrus zest is the colored outermost layer of a lemon, lime, or orange. It is best removed before you squeeze the fruit for the juice. First scrub the fruit in water to get rid of as much pesticide residue as possible and then peel with a grater, vegetable peeler, or citrus zester. Do not include any of the bitter white pith beneath the skin.

Apricot-Filled Oatmeal Bars

A kid pleaser, these bars can easily be made with your favorite preserves . . . try raspberry next time.

1½   cups flour
1½   cups quick-cooking or old-fashioned oats
¾   cup packed brown sugar
½   teaspoon baking soda
½   cup low-fat buttermilk
⅓   cup canola oil
1   (10-ounce) jar all-fruit apricot preserves

Combine the flour, oats, brown sugar and baking soda in a bowl and mix well. Add the buttermilk and canola oil and stir until combined; mixture will appear slightly dry.

Press ¾ of the oat mixture over the bottom of a 9x13-inch baking pan sprayed with nonstick cooking spray. Spread with the preserves. Sprinkle with the remaining oat mixture. Bake at 350 degrees for 20 to 25 minutes or until the edges pull from the sides of the pan. Let stand until cool. Cut into bars.

YIELD: 36 BARS

Nutrients Per Bar: Cal 89; Prot 1 g; Carbo 16 g; T Fat 2 g; (Saturated Fat <1 g); Chol <1 mg; Fiber 1 g; Sod 23 mg

Fruit purées can be substituted for some or all of the butter or oil in many baked goods. Prune purée works well in chocolate products, while unsweetened applesauce works well in baked goods requiring a more subtle flavor. Jars of baby food prunes are easy to use in recipes or you can make your own purée. →

Low-Fat Brownies

1½   cups flour
¾   cup baking cocoa
1   teaspoon baking powder
½   teaspoon salt
2¼   cups sugar
2   tablespoons margarine, softened
3   egg whites
¾   cup prune purée (see sidebar on page 202)
1   teaspoon vanilla extract

Sift or stir the flour, baking cocoa, baking powder and salt in a bowl. Beat the sugar and margarine in a mixer bowl until blended. Beat in the egg whites, prune purée and vanilla. Add the flour mixture, stirring just until moistened.

Spread the batter in a 9x13-inch baking pan sprayed with nonstick cooking spray. Bake at 350 degrees for 24 to 28 minutes or until a wooden pick inserted in the center comes out clean. Cool in pan on a wire rack. Cut into bars.

YIELD: 24 BROWNIES

Nutrients Per Brownie: Cal 137; Prot 2 g; Carbo 31 g; T Fat 1 g; (Saturated Fat <1 g); Chol 0 mg; Fiber 1 g; Sod 89 mg

For prune purée, combine 1⅓ cups pitted prunes (also known as dried plums) and ⅓ cup hot water in a food processor or blender container. Process until smooth. This makes about 1 cup and can be stored in the refrigerator for up to 1 month.

Continental Divide Hiking Bars

This recipe freezes well, so double it and have plenty on hand for your next outing.

⅓	cup sesame seeds
⅓	cup chopped sunflower kernels
⅓	cup chopped blanched almonds
⅓	cup chopped pecans or walnuts
⅓	cup unsweetened shredded coconut
3½	cups crisp rice cereal
1	cup dried cranberries
3	tablespoons peanut butter
2	tablespoons margarine
1	(10-ounce) package miniature marshmallows

Heat a large nonstick skillet over medium heat. Add the sesame seeds, sunflower kernels, almonds and pecans. Cook for 3 minutes or until lightly toasted, stirring constantly. Stir in the coconut. Cook for 2 minutes longer or until the coconut is golden brown. Remove from heat. Stir in the cereal and cranberries.

Combine the peanut butter, margarine and marshmallows in a large nonstick saucepan. Cook over low heat for 5 minutes or until smooth, stirring frequently. Remove from heat. Add the cereal mixture and mix well.

Spoon the cereal mixture into a 9x13-inch dish coated with nonstick cooking spray. Cover with foil. Using potholders to protect your hands, press firmly to make an even layer; discard the foil. Let stand until cool. Cut into 1½x3-inch bars. Store in an airtight container.

YIELD: 24 BARS

Nutrients Per Bar: Cal 153; Prot 3 g; Carbo 19 g; T Fat 8 g; (Saturated Fat 2 g); Chol 0 mg; Fiber 2 g; Sod 69 mg

Lemon Bars

1½   cups flour
½   cup rolled oats
½   cup confectioners' sugar
¼   teaspoon salt
⅔   cup low-fat buttermilk
3   tablespoons butter, melted
4   eggs, beaten
1½   cups sugar
⅓   cup fresh lemon juice
¼   cup flour
2   teaspoons finely grated lemon zest
      confectioners' sugar to taste

Combine 1½ cups flour, oats, ½ cup confectioners' sugar and salt in a bowl and mix well. Add the buttermilk and butter, stirring until a thick dough forms. Press over the bottom of a 9x13-inch baking pan sprayed with nonstick cooking spray. Bake at 350 degrees for 15 minutes.

Whisk the eggs, sugar, lemon juice, ¼ cup flour and lemon zest in a bowl. Pour over the hot baked layer. Bake for 20 minutes longer. Cool in pan on a wire rack. Sprinkle with confectioners' sugar to taste. Cut into 1x2-inch bars.

YIELD: 54 BARS

Nutrients Per Bar: Cal 56; Prot 1 g; Carbo 11 g; T Fat 1 g; (Saturated Fat 1 g); Chol 18 mg; Fiber <1 g; Sod 25 mg

To obtain the most juice from a lemon, allow the lemon to come to room temperature and then roll on a hard surface, pressing with the palm of your hand, before squeezing.

Key Lime Pie

1	envelope unflavored gelatin
¼	cup water
1	(14-ounce) can fat-free sweetened condensed milk
1	cup plain fat-free yogurt
½	cup Key lime juice
1	(9-inch) reduced-fat graham cracker pie shell

Sprinkle the gelatin over the water in a small saucepan. Let stand for 2 minutes to soften. Cook over low heat for 1 minute or just until the gelatin dissolves, stirring constantly. Cool slightly.

Whisk the condensed milk, yogurt and lime juice in a bowl until blended. Add the gelatin mixture and mix well. Spoon into the pie shell. Chill, covered, until set or preferably overnight. Garnish with fresh lime slices.

YIELD: 6 SERVINGS

Nutrients Per Serving: Cal 344; Prot 10 g; Carbo 66 g; T Fat 4 g; (Saturated Fat 1 g); Chol 5 mg; Fiber <1 g; Sod 221 mg

Pumpkin Pie in a Snap

2   cups crumbled gingersnap cookies
1   egg white
1   (16-ounce) can pumpkin
1   (12-ounce) can evaporated skim milk
½   cup egg whites (about 4 whites)
½   cup sugar
1   tablespoon pumpkin pie spice

Pour the crumbled gingersnap cookies into a blender or food processor container. Pulse until finely ground. Add 1 egg white. Pulse until combined. Press the crumb mixture using the back of a large spoon over the bottom and up the side of a 9-inch glass pie plate sprayed with nonstick cooking spray.

Whisk the pumpkin, evaporated skim milk, ½ cup egg whites, sugar and pumpkin pie spice in a bowl until blended. Spoon into the prepared pie plate. Bake at 350 degrees for 35 to 45 minutes or until a wooden pick inserted in the center comes out clean.

YIELD: 8 SERVINGS

Nutrients Per Serving: Cal 221; Prot 8 g; Carbo 42 g; T Fat 3 g; (Saturated Fat 1 g); Chol 2 mg; Fiber 3 g; Sod 255 mg

Canned evaporated skim milk, not to be confused with sweetened condensed milk, is a great substitution for cream in custard-type desserts and puddings. Because sixty percent of the water has been removed, evaporated skim milk provides a rich, creamy texture without adding additional fat. Ounce for ounce evaporated skim milk provides twice the calcium of skim milk or whole milk.

TESTERS AND CONTRIBUTORS

Rosanne Ainscough
Shannon Allen
Danette Anderson
Jean Anderson
Mike Anderson
Tami Anderson
Elizabeth Arvidson
Charlotte Bagwell
Doris Baker
Judy Barbe
Betsy Barringer
Carol Battalora
Naomi Benell
Anne Bennett
Mary Bennett
Jacqueline Berning
Kathleen Boland
Jenifer Bowman
Vivian Bradford
Laura Brieser-Smith
Deborah Broberg
Betty Brown
Kathy Brunner
Monica Burck
Marilynn Burger
Debbie Burton
Eva Byron
Lori Careswell
Jean Cassidy
Cherie Chao
Mary Lee Chin
Ada Clark
Amelia Cobb

Kevin Ann Conger
Anjenette Cooper
Laurie Coryell
Andrea Creager
Brenda Davy
Kathy Dechtman
Jennifer Dellaport
Katherine Delost-Lewis
Jennifer Dere
Lynn Dillon
Helen Dorrough
Susan Drake
Andrea L. Dunham
Julie Dutton
Susan Eckhardt
Barbara Eldridge
Carol Emich
Yasko Endo
Karen Erickson
Randy Erickson
Jamie Erskine
Lyndon Fallat
Melanie Faught
Shannon Fendler
Diana Ferriola
Cindi Fiechtner
Roz Fowler
Kathy Freidig
Joan Friend
Heidi Fritz
Sherrie Frye
Barb Gardner
Margaret Gasta

Natalie Gennett
Tracy Gillespie
Susan Gills
Geri Grange
Nanci Grayson
Marlene Griffith
Amy Halvorson-Bayer
Susan Hamilton
Carolyn Hammond
Sarah Harding Laidlaw
Mary Harris
Karen Hayes
Star Heintz
Laureen Heising
DeAnn Whitmire Hewett
Kathy Heyl
Beverly Hilleary
Anne Mary Hines
Ellen Hird
Joanne Holden
Sandy Holmes
Lilly Huppert
Cathy Jahde
Ann Johnsen
Candace Johnson
Mary Lu Jones
Lois Jorgenson
Pat Kelley
Karri Kent
Karla Klemm
Amelia Knezevich
Eve Knight
Rebecca Knight

TESTERS AND CONTRIBUTORS

Kathleen Koehler
Mary Koltze
Linda Kwiatkowski
Merna Kybic
Felice Larsen
Kathleen Lee
Kris Lenczycki
Susan Leonard
Kathy Lewis
Michelle Liebig
Shirley Lippincott
Sharon Lloyd
Lyndy Lubbers
Anne Luhr
Nancy Macey
Melony Major
Liz Marr
Robynn Martinson
Suzanne Mason
Kay Massey
Judy Matthews
Kathryn McClain
Teresa McFee
Cathie McKibbon
Helen McLaughlin
Marty Meitus
Carol Miller
Erin Murray
Sherri Orrison
Denise Palmeri
Beth Pannbacker
Alice Parker
Lucille Patterson

Karen Payne
Jo Ann Pegues
Paula Peirce
Kristiana Petre
Cynthia Phillips
Lisa Poggas
Nancy Pudwill
Joanne Randolph
Catherine Reade
Gina Rickhoff
Marilyn Rickson
Shirley Rieke
Norma Robinson
Chris Rock
Mary Rock
Marian Ruge
Katie Ryan
Terri Ryan-Turek
Colleen Schneckenburger
Mary Schroeder
Maureen Scott
Melanie Sedbrook
David Seddon
Mary Sinkay
Teresa Skinner O'Clair
Barbara Skolnick-
   Schwartz
Jennifer Smith
Laine Smith
Scott Smith
Stephanie Smith
Susan Smith
Parolea Soggin

Peg Spangler
Pat Spellman
Maureen Sprague
Linda Staples
Jeni Stem
Susan Stevens
Amy Suyama
Sally Swartz
Helen Thompson
Lyn Thor
Terry Tusberg
Lynn Umbreit
Katie Vogel
Jean Wagenaar
Brenda Walker
Shawna Walker
Alisson Waltman
Laura Watne
Diane Wenzel
Carrie Wheeler
Heather Wheeler
Kim Whittington
Kaia Wilkinson
Kristine Wolfe
Marge Wylie
Clara Zerbe

EQUIVALENT CHART

WHEN THE RECIPE CALLS FOR   **USE**

Baking
1/2 cup butter . . . . 4 ounces
2 cups butter . . . . 1 pound
4 cups all-purpose flour . . . . 1 pound
1 square chocolate . . . . 1 ounce
1 cup semisweet chocolate chips . . . . 6 ounces
2 1/4 cups packed brown sugar . . . . 1 pound
4 cups confectioners' sugar . . . . 1 pound
2 cups granulated sugar . . . . 1 pound

Cereal/Bread
1 cup fine dry bread crumbs . . . . 4 to 5 slices
1 cup soft bread crumbs . . . . 2 slices
1 cup fine cracker crumbs . . . . 28 saltines
1 cup vanilla wafer crumbs . . . . 22 wafers
1 cup crushed cornflakes . . . . 3 cups, uncrushed
4 cups cooked macaroni . . . . 8 ounces, uncooked
3 1/2 cups cooked rice . . . . 1 cup, uncooked

Dairy
1 cup shredded cheese . . . . 4 ounces
1 cup cottage cheese . . . . 8 ounces
2/3 cup evaporated milk . . . . 1 small can
1 2/3 cups evaporated milk . . . . 1 (13-ounce) can

Fruit
4 cups sliced or chopped apples . . . . 4 medium
1 cup mashed bananas . . . . 3 medium
3 to 4 tablespoons lemon juice plus 1 tablespoon grated lemon zest . . . . 1 lemon
1/3 cup orange juice plus 2 teaspoons grated orange zest . . . . 1 orange

Meats
4 cups chopped cooked chicken . . . . 1 (5-pound) chicken
3 cups chopped cooked meat . . . . 1 pound, cooked
2 cups cooked ground meat . . . . 1 pound, cooked

Vegetables
2 cups cooked green beans . . . . 1/2 pound fresh or 1 (16-ounce) can
2 1/2 cups lima beans or red beans . . . . 1 cup dried, cooked
4 cups shredded cabbage . . . . 1 pound
1 cup grated carrot . . . . 1 large
8 ounces fresh mushrooms . . . . 1 (4-ounce) can
1 cup chopped onion . . . . 1 large
4 cups sliced or chopped potatoes . . . . 4 medium
2 cups canned tomatoes . . . . 1 (16-ounce) can

Name of Recipe	Bread/ Starch	Other Carbs/Sugar	Very Lean Meat/Protein	Lean Meat	Fruit	Vegetable	Skim Milk	Fat
Appetizers								
Polenta Antipasto	1			0				0
Fresh Basil Bruschetta	.5			0		0		0
Hot Artichoke Crostini	.5	0		0		0		0
Sun-Dried Tomato Crostini	1		0			0		0
Crab Meat Canapés		0	.5		0	0		0
Snappy Black Bean Dip	0		.5	0		0		0
Hot Pepper Cheese Dip			.5	0		0	0	1
Five-Minute Pesto Dip				0		.5	0	.5
Southwestern Layered Dip	.5		.5	.5	0	.5		1.5
Caponata		0	0			.5		.5
Smoked Salmon Pâté	0	0	1	.5	0	0		1
Mushroom Pâté		0			0	.5		.5
Baked Chinese Dumplings	.3	0	0			0		0
Marinated Mushrooms	0	0		0		0		0
Cajun Shrimp	0	.5	2		0	0		0
Chinese Tortilla Roll-Ups	.5	0	.5			0		0
Brunch								
At-Home Cappuccino	0	0					.5	
Palisade Peach Smoothie	1.5				5.5			
Fruit with Orange Yogurt Dip		1			1			0
The Best Granola	1.5	1		1	1			5
Mexicana Cheese Pie	1	0	1			0		1
Omelet Sandwiches On-The-Run	2		1	1		.5	0	1
Miner's Potato and Ham Frittata	1		2	1		0		1.5
Tofu Breakfast Scramble	0		1	.5		.5		1
Alpine Baked Oatmeal	2	1		0	.5		0	.5
Baked Breakfast Apples	1	2.5			2.5			0
Cinnamon Bubble Bread	1.5	1					0	0
Pear Walnut Coffee Cake	.5	1		0	.5			1.5
Raspberry Almond Coffee Cake	1	1		0	0		0	1
Banana-Stuffed French Toast	4	.5	.5	.5	1		0	.5
Buttermilk Pancakes with Good Morning Mango Sauce	1	.5	0		.5		0	.5

Name of Recipe	Bread/ Starch	Other Carbs/Sugar	Very Lean Meat/Protein	Lean Meat	Fruit	Vegetable	Skim Milk	Fat
Granolaberry Pancakes	1.5	0		0	0		0	1
Trailside Multigrain Pancakes	1.5	0	0	0	0		0	0
Soups and Salads								
Creamy Artichoke Soup	.5			1		3	.5	1
Snowy Weekend Cassoulet	2		3			1		.5
Tasty Turkey Chili	1	0		2.5		3		.5
Hearty White Chili	.5		2.5	.5		.5		1
Cheddar Chicken Chowder	1.5		2	.5		1	.5	1
Greek Lemon Chicken Soup	1		.5	1	0			.5
Southwestern Chicken Soup	2		3.5	1		1		0
Autumn Curry Soup	1.5			1		0		.5
Creamy Curry Onion Soup	.5			1		1.5		.5
Hot and Sour Soup	.5	.5	1	1		.5		.5
Spicy African Rice and Peanut Stew	2			.5		1		1
Mexican Tomato Soup with Lime		.5			0	2		0
Wild Rice and Chicken Soup	2		3.5	.5		.5	1	1.5
Seafood Chowder			3			2		1.5
Vegetable Lentil Soup	2		0			2.5		0
Creamy Fruit and Nut Medley	0	.5		0	3	.5		.5
Marinated Beet Salad		0			0	2.5		
Curry Broccoli Potato Salad	1	0				.5	0	.5
Steak and Roasted Vegetable Salad	0	0		3		3.5		
Raspberry Chicken Salad		2	7	1		.5		.5
Imperial Krab Salad	1		2.5	0		1.5	0	1
Dilled Shrimp and Rice	2.5	0	1	0	0	0		1.5
Tuna Summer Salad			2.5			.5	0	.5
Spicy Black Bean Salsa Salad	2	0	1		0	.5		.5
Parmesan Pasta and Bean Salad	2	0	.5	0		1	0	1.5
Asiago Pasta Salad	2			.5		2		1
Crunchy Pea and Cashew Salad	.5	.5		0		.5	0	.5
San Juan Salad with Creamy Tofu Dressing	2	0	0			.5		0
Strawberry Spinach Salad		1			0	.5		1
Spinach Potluck Salad		.5		0		1		1.5
Mixed Greens with Herbed Merlot Dressing			.5			.5		1.5
Mixed Greens with Pears, Bleu Cheese and Pecans	0	0		.5	1	.5		2
Garlic Caesar Salad	.5	0		0		1		1.5

Name of Recipe	Bread/Starch	Other Carbs/Sugar	Very Lean Meat/Protein	Lean Meat	Fruit	Vegetable	Skim Milk	Fat
Entrées								
Mongolian Beef	2.5	.5		3.5		0		0
Citrus-Grilled Flank Steak		0	3.5		.5			2
Grilled Steak Bruschetta	3			3		.5		1
Beef Burgundy	.5		4.5			.5		2
Savory Stuffed Peppers Italian-Style	1	0	1	0		2.5		0
Spinach Enchilada Casserole	1	0	1	2	0	1		1.5
Teriyaki Miniature Meat Loaves	0	1		2		0		1
Grilled Lamb with Garlic Rub	0			4.5	0			0
Jalapeño Honey Pork Tenderloin		1	3.5			.5		1
Grilled Pork Chops with Cherry Almond Sauce	0	2	3	0				1
Oriental Fruited Pork	2.5	0	2.5		1			1.5
Pork Souvlaki Kabobs			1.5		0	1		2.5
Mile-High Marinara and Prosciutto	2.5		1	.5		3		1
Home-Style Skillet Chicken	.5		6					2
Chicken Breasts with Herb Sauce	0		7	0		0		2
Chicken Oregano			7	0				1
Chicken Tortilla Casserole	2		2			1.5		1.5
Herb Mustard Grilled Chicken		0	7	0		0		1
Lemon Chicken with Fettuccini	2	0	3.5	0		0		1
Plum-Glazed Chicken Kabobs	0	1.5	4			.5		.5
Baked Sour Cream Chicken	1	0	7					.5
Thai Chicken and Noodles	1.5	0	2	0		.5		1
Vegetable Chicken Lasagna	.5		3.5	2		3		1
Cranberry Chicken and Wild Rice	2.5	0	7	0	2			1
Ginger Chicken Wraps	4	.5	3			1		1.5
Peppery Turkey Breast with Pineapple Cranberry Relish		2	8		1			
Orange Roughy Mediterranean-Style			3		0	2		1
Salmon Loaf	0	0		2.5	0	1	0	1
Salmon en Papillote		.5		5		1		.5
Glazed Salmon		1		4.5				
Stuffed Fish Rolls		0	2.5		0	1		.5
Pesto Swordfish		0	3.5	.5		1		2
Pumpkin Seed Trout	1		3.5			1.5	.5	1.5
Fish Tacos	1.5	0	2		0	0	0	3

Name of Recipe	Bread/Starch	Other Carbs/Sugar	Very Lean Meat/Protein	Lean Meat	Fruit	Vegetable	Skim Milk	Fat
Balsamic-Glazed Tuna	0	.5	5.5	0		0		1
Grilled Tuna with Strawberry Salsa		0	5.5		.5	0		1.5
Linguini with Red Clam Sauce	3		0	0		1		.5
Shrimp and Scallop Kabobs	0	0	3		.5	1		.5
Spicy Shrimp Paella	3	0	1.5	.5		.5		.5
Meatless Entrées								
Black Bean Tortilla Casserole	2.5		2			2.5	0	1
Cowgirl Beans	2	0	0			2		0
Boulder Burritos	3.5		.5		0	2		2
Sesame Chick-Pea Dinner Wraps	4	0		.5	0	.5		2
Portobello Florentine	0			.5		3		.5
Portobello Mushroom Stir-Fry	3	0				1		0
Grilled Portobello Mushroom Sandwiches	2.5	.5		.5		2		1.5
Layered Rigatoni Bake	1		1	1		2.5		1.5
Long-Life Noodles	3.5	0		.5		1		1.5
Spiced Lentils over Pasta	3.5	0	1			1.5	0	1
Spinach Quesadillas	2	0		0		1.5		0
Cranberry-Glazed Tempeh	1	.5		2.5	2.5	0		0
Grilled Tofu Steaks	0	0	1					1
Telluride Tofu and Mushrooms	3	.5	1			1		1
Vegetable Tofu Curry	1	0	.5		1	1.5		1
Vegetable Barley Bake	3		1	.5		1		1
Vegetables, Grains and Pasta								
Roasted Artichokes					0	3		1
Awesome Asparagus		0		0		1		1
Broccoli Dijon		0				.5		.5
Maple-Glazed Carrots		0			0	1		0
Cauliflower in Spicy Tomato Sauce		0				3		
Stuffed Eggplant Mediterranean-Style	.5			.5		3.5		1
Potatoes in Wine	1.5	0				0		1
Mountain Mashers	1.5	0					0	1
Rosemary Potatoes	2					0		.5
Roasted Root Vegetables						4		.5
Sautéed Spinach with Corn Relish	.5	0				1		0
Summer Squash and Mushroom Bake	0			.5		1		.5
Praline Sweet Potato Casserole	2	1.5		.5				1

Name of Recipe	Bread/ Starch	Other Carbs/Sugar	Very Lean Meat/Protein	Lean Meat	Fruit	Vegetable	Skim Milk	Fat
Washington Park Sweet Potatoes with Tart Cherries	1	.5			1.5			.5
Sweet Potato Chips	1.5					0		.5
Crispy Zucchini Coins	1		.5	.5				0
Fire-Grilled Vegetables	0	0				1		0
High Country Vegetable Bake				0		2		0
Barley and Pine Nuts	1.5		0	0		.5		1
Zucchini Couscous	1	0				0		.5
Savory Polenta	1			0		0		.5
Cinnamon Brown Rice	1.5			0	.5			.5
Confetti Rice	1.5					1		
La Junta Lentils and Rice	4		.5	.5		.5		.5
Pecan Rice	3.5			.5		.5		2
Microwave Risotto	2.5			.5		.5		1
Fresh Tomato Pesto over Angel Hair Pasta	2		0	.5		1.5		2
Pasta with Beer Cheese Sauce	2.5		1			1	0	1
Lemon Caper Orzo	1.5				0	0		0
Mushroom and Pine Nut Pasta Sauce	0		0			2		1
Breads and Pizza								
Colorado Gold Corn Bread	2	0		.5		0	0	.5
Flatirons Flatbread	2	0	0					.5
Lemon Poppy Seed Bread	1	1.5		0	0	0	0	.5
Harvest Pumpkin Bread	1.5	1		0	0			1
Applesauce Bran Muffins	1	1		0	.5			1
Banana Chocolate Chip Muffins	1	1	0	0	.5		0	1
Cinnamon Corn Muffins	1	0		0	0		0	.5
Cranberry Muffins	1	1		0	0		0	1
Pumpkin Walnut Muffins	1	.5	0	0	.5		0	1
Apricot Scones	1.5	.5			.5		0	1
Orange Cranberry Scones	1	.5					0	.5
Frijol Pizza	5	0	1	1		0		1.5
Southwest Beef and Chile Pizza	3.5	0	.5	2		1		1
Barbecue Chicken Pizza	3.5	.5	3.5	1		0		1
Veggie Pita Pizzas	1.5		.5			1		2
Crusty Whole Wheat Pizza Crust	16.5		0					2
Grilled Garlic Herb Pizza Crust	2.5	0	0			0		.5
Desserts								
Cappuccino Cheesecake	0	1.5	1	0				1
Caramel Bananas		2.5			2.5			1

Name of Recipe	Bread/ Starch	Other Carbs/Sugar	Very Lean Meat/Protein	Lean Meat	Fruit	Vegetable	Skim Milk	Fat
Gingered Peaches		1		.5	1.5	0		1
Poached Pears in Spiced Red Wine Sauce	.5	2			2			1.5
Cranapple Crisp	1	1			2			0
Fanciful Pudding		1.5			1		.5	0
Speedy Rice Pudding	1.5	1		0	.5		.5	0
Light Tiramisù	0	1		0				2.5
Fresh Strawberry Torte	.5	1	.5	0	.5			1
Applesauce Spice Cake	1	2	.5	0	1		0	.5
Fluffy Cream Cheese Frosting		1		0				.5
Triple-Chocolate Bundt Cake		2.5	0	0			0	1.5
Chocolate Yogurt Cake	1	1.5	0	0			0	1
Banana Strawberry Frozen Yogurt		1			1		.5	
Almond Spice Biscotti	.5	0	0	0	0			.5
Brownie Oat Chews	.5	.5	0					0
Outrageous Orange Cookies	0	.5		0	0		0	.5
Apricot-Filled Oatmeal Bars	.5	1					0	.5
Low-Fat Brownies	.5	1	0		.5			0
Continental Divide Hiking Bars	0	1	0	0	0			1.5
Lemon Bars	0	.5		0	0		0	0
Key Lime Pie		4	0				0	1
Pumpkin Pie in a Snap	1	2	.5	0			.5	0

INDEX

Simply Colorado, *Too!*

Simply Colorado, Inc.
4945 Meade Street • Denver, Colorado 80221-1031
Phone (720) 855-8652 • Fax (303) 561-0369
www.eatrightcolorado.org

Please send me _____ copies of *Simply* Colorado, *Too!* at $19.95 per book $ _____

Postage and handling at $3.00 per book $ _____

Denver-Metro residents add $1.46 sales tax per book $ _____

Colorado residents outside Denver-Metro add $.60 sales tax per book $ _____

Total $ _____

Name _____

Address _____ Phone _____

City _____ State _____ Zip _____

Make checks payable to Simply Colorado, Inc. Please do not send cash. Sorry, no CODs.

Profits from the sale of this cookbook are used to support the purpose
and programs of the Colorado Dietetic Association.

Simply Colorado, *Too!*

Simply Colorado, Inc.
4945 Meade Street • Denver, Colorado 80221-1031
Phone (720) 855-8652 • Fax (303) 561-0369
www.eatrightcolorado.org

Please send me _____ copies of *Simply* Colorado, *Too!* at $19.95 per book $ _____

Postage and handling at $3.00 per book $ _____

Denver-Metro residents add $1.46 sales tax per book $ _____

Colorado residents outside Denver-Metro add $.60 sales tax per book $ _____

Total $ _____

Name _____

Address _____ Phone _____

City _____ State _____ Zip _____

Make checks payable to Simply Colorado, Inc. Please do not send cash. Sorry, no CODs.

Profits from the sale of this cookbook are used to support the purpose
and programs of the Colorado Dietetic Association.

Photocopies will be accepted.